Nothing

True unsolicited comments from readers:

"I was truly moved and changed by reading this book. I have been on the path for a number of years reading all kinds of books, and *Nothing* is the best...truly beyond words."

—*JLS, Utah*

"I have read *Nothing* several times now and think it is the best book of its type that I have ever read."

—*EW, New Jersey*

"I get great pleasure from *Nothing*. I open it often to remind myself of the truths therein."

—*VB, Chicago*

"*Nothing* is the best book I've read in a long time...a beautiful job."

—*SG, Phoenix*

"*Nothing* came as we were experiencing an unusually tough situation...it helped immensely."

—*J&PS, Miami*

"I have read extensively in this area but had not previously encountered a work wherein clarity of vision and uncluttered sensibility were so evenly balanced...*Nothing* speaks straight to the heart...it's helping so much."

—*VL, N. Carolina*

This book is graced with the wonderful
drawings of the artist Tonia Weeks,
who may be contacted at 919-682-3924

Nothing
2ND EDITION

James Sloman

OceanBlue
PUBLISHING
TIBURON, CALIFORNIA

To order this book
or any OceanBlue product
call anytime 1-800-838-7360

OceanBlue Publishing
98 Main St, Tiburon, CA 94920
www.ocean-blue.com

Contents

 *Foreword*

Nothing was originally published in 1981.

For this new second edition an extensive revision was undertaken, but an attempt was made also to retain the basic essence and flavor of the original book.

Nothing has the grand certainty of youth—I was 37 at the time—but from my current vantage point that seems like one of its charms.

Currently, it's increasingly clear that I know nothing at all about anything at all, least of all about anything discussed in this book. And I like that.

Adapted from the Foreword in 1981:

This book is the result of an experience in March of 1980 which did not bring about mastery but did bring a clear glimpse of an alternate reality, or rather, an alternate way of perceiving this reality.

In order to communicate about this experience, stories and concepts from various sources have been used. The work of such benefactors to humanity as Jesus, the Buddha, Byron Katie, Osho, Lao-Tzu, etc. has been very influential.

I've also been influenced by other teachers such as Ram Dass, Werner Erhard, Ken Keyes Jr., Mahaghossananda, my friend Richard Gobeille, and many others.

This book was originally made possible by the gracious assistance of Howard Brown, Carol Schroeder, John Weeks, the late and great Alfred Kapuler, and others.

More recently, I would also like to thank these heartful people: Bill Anderson, Rebecca Bell, RayAnn Burnham, Tom and Nilza Kallos, John Keiser, Peggy MacKay, Dan Marcellus, Mary Poling, Van and Kala Tharp, Franz Wanowitz, David Waterhouse, Caroline Whitehead, Tom Zagara and especially Carroll Stephenson. And many others. Thank you all.

A special gratitude to my former wife Tonia Weeks, my mother Ann Romanchuck and my associate JoAnne Munley for their great open hearts.

I would like to express my special appreciation in this book to Osho. He had a profoundly beneficial impact on my early life, and I'd like to acknowledge my special indebtedness to him. I've tried to incorporate here wherever possible his beautiful metaphors about the Mystery.

I would like finally to express my gratitude to the many people who cannot be named here and who have touched my life in profound ways. Thank you all so much.

Last, I would like to acknowledge the countless people in all ages and situations who have labored mightily, most of them in obscurity, to benefit their corner of the world. You are all an inspiration.

Everything said here has been said many times before, in many different ways over thousands of years. I hope you might find useful this particular arrangement and expression of what has gone before.

The Mind

 *Chapter One*

A true story...

It concerns Alexander the Great, the world conqueror, and Diogenes, a mystic who lived in Athens during the fourth century BC. Diogenes possessed nothing except for a begging bowl, and one day he threw even that small possession away. Diogenes was well known then for his serene, blissful state. Alexander had heard of him and desired to meet him.

It's one of the more interesting meetings in history. Diogenes was sunning himself alongside a river bank as the conqueror approached. Alexander looked into those silent, blissful eyes and told Diogenes that he greatly admired him, and then asked if there was anything he could do for him.

Diogenes paused a moment, and then said, "Yes, there is one thing you could do for me. You could move a little to the side, you're blocking the sun."

An eerie and beautiful reply. The most powerful man in the world was offering anything, and Diogenes asked him not to block the sun. Here was a person who needed nothing.

Alexander said, "When I am finished conquering the world I am going to come and join you on the river bank and just relax."

Diogenes replied, "There is no need to conquer the world first. I have not conquered the world and I am relaxing. What is preventing you? You can relax now."

Alexander said, "No, I must conquer the world first."

Then Diogenes said to him, "You will never finish. You will die in the middle of it." And Alexander did indeed. In the midst of a war campaign he died.

This is our mind, always needing to do something first before it can relax. In fact, it can never relax because it is always occupied. The mind's disease is constant occupation. If the mind stops being occupied it simply ceases to exist. It is like a shark, which must stay moving to breathe. Without movement the mind will die.

Even to say it will die is incorrect, because the very movement *is* the mind. It is not the shark but the movement itself. When the movement stops, the mind is already gone because it never actually existed. But the movement—mind's constant occupation—made it seem as if it did.

And with what is the mind occupied? With thoughts, emotions, sensations, desires, goals, problems, preferences, activities and so on. Anything at all that is said or done or felt or thought is of the mind. It is all mind, and mind is always in movement. The mind can be compared to a dance. There is no dance apart from the movement, and the moment the movement stops there is no dance.

It looks as if there are many problems in our lives. But the masters say there is only one: the mind. There is only that one problem, they say, and if that problem is solved then all other problems are solved instantly, they simply cease to exist, because they never existed in the first place apart from the problem of mind itself. Mind created all our problems, they say, and no matter how many problems we solve more will appear unless we solve the basic problem of mind itself.

It's like a tree where we're cutting off leaves one by one, solving one problem after another. But we're surprised, too, because for every leaf we cut off three more appear. Every gardener knows that the way to thicken a tree is to prune it. Thus for every problem we solve others appear; the process never ends. We become exhausted solving this never-ending series of problems.

If we look deeply enough, we'll see that the process will *never* end; new leaves will always keep growing. So we must look not to the leaves but to the root—the mind—for that is where the real problem resides. If we cut the root all the leaves will wither simultaneously.

So let's look to the root, not to the leaves. Let's look to the nature of mind itself.

 *Chapter Two*

What is this nature? It is the nature of mind to always seek, to want. It is a pursuer, a goal-seeking mechanism. It is always trying to get somewhere; that is why it is never here. Look at the way we talk to ourselves: "Once I get the right partner, then everything will be fine." "As soon as I get the new raise, then I can relax." "Once the addition is on the house, then I can really enjoy myself." "Once I get over the hump with this problem, then I'll be happy."

Our mind is always in the future, and it is never here. Happiness is always a goal a little way off that will be achieved when the problems are solved. But have we noticed? As soon as one problem is solved, others are there. As soon as one goal is reached there are new goals. It has to be so, for the mind is a goal-seeker. Without goals, without desires it cannot exist. It must have movement, it must have something to go toward. That is its nature.

Then we might ask, what is a problem to this mind? A problem is anything that the mind cannot accept. It's the mind's desire for something or other to be different than the way it is. It's some situation inconsistent with the mind's model of how the situation *should* be.

If we have no desire for anything to be different than it is, there's no problem. But the mind always has a list of things which it wants to be different; hence it always has many problems to solve. This keeps it occupied; it keeps it alive.

What is the ultimate problem the mind is working on? Its ultimate problem is death. The mind does not want to be annihilated, and it remains in fear because it knows that death can come at any time. If we look deeply inside we can see a trembling, a tension—the fear of annihilation. The mind is constantly working on the problem of how to survive. Its goal is to find a way to keep on existing, forever if possible.

To assuage this inner fear mind tries to gather more and more security, power and pleasure. Mind becomes a collector. It collects more status, prestige, wealth, possessions. It collects more knowledge, more data, more answers. It collects more sensations, and then more yet. More food or more sex or more adventure. More partners, friends or allies. More technology. More houses or cars or clothes or books, more experiences, more solutions. Each of us is different but each of us wants more of something. It's the nature of the mind.

But no amount of more, no amount of collecting will satisfy the fear and trembling because all collecting is outer and the fear and trembling are inner. And this outer can never satisfy the inner. That's why the mind is greedy. It gathers more and more, hoping to fill the inner hollowness, but it can never fill it, and so it goes on gathering, wanting, seeking. The game never ends, it goes on until the day of death. We always die in the middle—in the middle of getting what we want.

 *Chapter Three*

The mind has been compared to a drunken monkey swinging through the trees, for its incessant activity never stops. Look at a monkey; it's always doing something. It fidgets, it scratches, it eats, it looks around; it never stops except when it sleeps. Now look at the thoughts of our mind, they have the same quality. Our mind flies from one thing to another endlessly. "The table...made of hard wood...where does it come from?...Oregon, I imagine...I wonder what it would be like to live there...I hear it's rainy...we've certainly had very little rain here recently...the farmers need some rain ...that's a hard life, farming..." And on it goes.

Incessant thought is manifested in incessant activity. Even during relaxation we often stay active: chewing gum, leafing through a magazine, listening to the radio, cooking, snacking, reading, watching TV. To the mind the question is always, "What's next?" And so we go from eating to talking to working to making love to reading to watching a movie to going to the beach to eating to going to a party...forever.

"What's next?" The mind gets a gratification moment, but then the moment passes and the mind wants another. It gets another and that passes too; then it wants yet another, ad infinitum. The mind can never be in the present because to the mind the present is only a means to an end.

This is why the mind is always essentially in misery, because it can never be here in the present moment.

Our mind's pictures of what we're supposed to do are based on memories from the past. It uses the past to try to get to the future. Since the mind is always in in the past or future, it has to be mostly miserable.

Misery is just another name for never being here now, always being somewhere other than where we are. The misery is pushed down so we won't notice it too much, but it's always there. Even when we're seemingly feeling good, deep down the buried misery remains.

It looks as if we're herenow, but almost always we're not. If we're washing dishes we're not just washing dishes. First we set up a short-term goal which we may not even notice—to get to the end of washing dishes. And we want to accomplish something by washing the dishes.

In the meantime we're thinking a thousand and one thoughts: what Bob said yesterday...the dinner we're going to have tonight...oh, the plants need watering...how beautiful Carrie is...but she likes the temperature of the house too high...on and on. And we're restimulated by the memory of when we were washing the dishes last year and burned our hand. We're not herenow.

The mind can never truly play, because playing is of the present, it hasn't any past or future in it. To have fun is to do something without having any goal in it, neither the goal of pleasure nor the goal of getting to the end of it. It's just play, frolic; there's no purpose to it.

True play is incomprehensible to the mind because to the mind everything must have a purpose, it must serve some end, it must have a meaning. Otherwise, what is the point? But fun and play have no point; that's their point. They're just what they are.

Osho tells the story of a seeker who was very good at archery. He would hit the target virtually every time. He went to Japan to study under an archery master, to get the certificate from him. In Japan they use all sorts of excuses to teach meditation. Archery is one of them. The seeker would hit the target again and again but the master would only say, "You are shooting the arrow. The arrow must shoot itself."

This sounds absurd. How can the arrow shoot itself? The seeker continued hitting the target. Then he attempted to deliberately *not* hit the target. That didn't work either. The master said, "The target is not the target. You are the target." The master wasn't interested in the end, the outcome. He was interested in the beginning.

The seeker couldn't get the certificate from the master, so after three years he gave up and packed his bags to return home. He went to say goodbye to the master, who was on the archery range.

The seeker sat down to watch and now he was no longer interested in the certificate; he had given that up.

And he saw the master for the first time. The master was just having fun; there was nobody interested in hitting the target. The seeker then took the bow and pulled back the arrow. He was no longer concerned, he was just playing now. Before the arrow had left the bow the master turned away and said, "Finished. The target has been reached."

Deep down, our minds are always serious, always trying to reach to the target. Mind can't understand that the target is already here because its very nature is to be striving to reach the target.

Thus the mind is almost always involved in struggle, in trying. It's always making an effort, involved in difficulties and obstacles.

The mind never sees that this endless seeking is the real problem. It never sees that its attempts to find a solution are the very motions that keep it from seeing that no solution is necessary. It's like a muddy pond where our motion in the pond to clear up the mud is the very thing that keeps the water muddy and prevents us from seeing beneath the surface to the mysterious bottom.

 *Chapter Four*

The basis of the mind's motion towards all its goals is discriminations. The world is a totality but the mind separates it into a multiplicity through its labels, concepts, categories. The mind is a labeler and labels everything. "This is a tree, that is a fence. This is moving, that is stationary. This is red, that is orange. He is well-dressed, she is average. The boy is good-looking, his father is not. This is a cloudy day, too bad, yesterday was sunny."

Mind then perceives reality through its constructs and concepts rather than directly. Experiments have indicated that a person shown a red ace of spades will see an ace of hearts, because he has a concept that red means a heart or diamond. Other experiments have shown that if by prearrangement a crowd of people claims to see something that isn't there then the uninitiated observer will see it too. They will actually see something that isn't there because the mind computes that it must be there.

In fact all labels, all concepts set up dualities. To create a category of "tree" we must simultaneously create a category of "not-tree," of all that which is not a tree. Otherwise this category of "tree" has no meaning. It's the same with all our categories. "Up" has no meaning without "down." Something can only be "up" in relation to something else which is "down." The two concepts come into being together. No "up" or "down" exists in reality. Such labels are mind-creations.

Similarly, "beautiful" can't exist without "ugly." "Good" cannot exist without "bad." It is all the mind's creation. The mind's experiences are determined by its theories, and in turn reinforce those theories.

Through some experience we set up a belief, let's say, that men with beards are impolite. And we find that every man with a beard follows the rule. We bring our expectation to each situation, and then we get to be right.

Mind wants to be right at all costs because the mind is a collection of points of view. Thus, being right about its point of view is tantamount to survival. And then when we come across a bearded man who is not impolite, we're still right, because he becomes "the exception that proves the rule." And the moment he slips up we say, "See? I knew I was right. Men with beards are impolite." Mind lives in its own reality.

There's an Hassidic story about this. There was a zaddic, an Hassidic master, who became a judge. Because he was very conscious he was not concerned with being right but saw rightness in everything. The first case came up and the judge heard the plaintiff and then said, "Right. You are right."

The court clerk took him aside and said, "Are you crazy? You have only heard one side; how can you pronounce it right?" The judge said, "You're right. Let's hear the defense." After hearing the defense the judge said, "Yes, right. You are absolutely right." The clerk took the judge aside again and said, "Now you are insane. You have done what you should never do, you have made both sides right." And the judge said, "Of course, you're right. How can both sides be right?"

This is the opposite of what the mind does. Mind clings to its point of view, it clings to its rightness. Mind is a clinger. As soon as it discriminates it starts preferring one thing to another. It makes a multiplicity out of the totality and then starts picking and choosing among the multiplicity. It prefers palm trees over fir trees, or vice-versa. It prefers blue over red, or tall women over short, or a big house over a small one, or prestige over disgrace, or whatever. Desire has arisen.

Now what exists in the moment is not enough. Now something must be obtained before the moment will be enough. And something else must be pushed away. Mind clings to what it likes and tries to avoid what it dislikes. It becomes attached to its desires, preferences, points of view, beliefs and goals. It clings to people, possessions, money, power, youth. It attaches itself to particular solutions, answers, rituals, habitual attitudes, ways of acting and models of how things should be. The mind becomes as brittle and rigid as a dead stick of wood. It loses the flexibility of life and becomes dead inside. But it continues to cling because it equates that with survival.

The most basic point of view that the mind has, the most basic duality that it creates, is that it is separate. This assumption is so fundamental that the mind cannot even see it as an assumption. It's like water to a fish. The mind sees this as simply one of the givens of existence. It doesn't question this paradigm because the paradigm runs so deep that it can't even be seen as a paradigm. Intellectually perhaps, yes; but at the level of blood and bone, no.

And this paradigm colors all of life. Naturally, since the mind feels separate it must struggle, strive, survive, and make things go right.

In fact, this whole question of rightness or wrongness is one of the most intriguing aspects of the mind. The mind sees many things as wrong because it sees many things as directly or indirectly threatening to its survival as a separate thing.

If somebody steals our computer it's "wrong" because the mind sees it as threatening to survival. If somebody or something is different from the model in our head then we call them or it "wrong."

All minds are ill, but a simple test of how much illness a mind has is to observe how much "complaint" it has.

 *Chapter Five*

One night as the master Shichiri Kojun was meditating a thief entered with a sword, demanding his money or his life. "Do not disturb me," the master said. "The money is in that drawer over there." The thief gathered the money and prepared to leave. "Remember to thank me," the master said. The thief thanked him and left.

Caught for other crimes, the thief confessed also to the burglary against the master. Called to testify and asked what happened, Shichiri said, "A man came and I gave him a gift of money. He thanked me and left. There was no thief."

Each of us creates our own reality by what we notice, by the concepts and interpretations that we overlay onto what is. Reality itself is not knowable by the mind. Our senses are small windows indeed. Our faculty of sight, for instance, is only a tiny segment of the whole electromagnetic spectrum.

And concerning the data that is available, our senses act to filter out most of it. For example, it's been demonstrated that a frog's eye notices only nearby movements characteristic of insects. All other visual data is screened out.

And what little data the brain does receive must then be interpreted by the brain before we experience the sensation of sight or any other sense. There is no way to know for sure that the brain is not manufacturing its product completely internally—and that what we think of as sense data may just be part of the internal computation.

In other words, we don't really know what's out there, we have actually no idea of what exists external to us. And there may be nothing at all out there; all of our sensory data may be a completely internal product of the brain. There's no way to be certain about it.

Yet all of our concepts, beliefs, opinions, knowledge are ultimately based upon sensory data. Reality in its ultimate essence simply cannot be known by the mind. Someone sits in a room, and in the same room an ant crawls across the floor. It perceives a totally different reality than the person does. Which reality is correct? Both. Neither. Neither perceives ultimate reality. Both have their own version.

The Taoist master Chuang Tzu said, "How can you talk about the sea to a frog in a well?" Mind is always in its own little well, hemmed in by its limited data and then hemming itself in further by the concepts and beliefs it forms about the data. Then those concepts, beliefs, attitudes, models and so on form the screen through which further data is perceived and interpreted. Mind lives in its well and thinks that its well is the totality. It thinks that its well is the way things really are, it thinks that its well is the sea itself.

Another way of looking at this is to see the mind as a projector which uses reality as merely a screen upon which to project its own version of things. Mind projects its fantasies, attitudes, concepts and models onto reality and then confuses this motion picture with reality itself.

Mind is a dreamer and it never stops dreaming even for a single moment. And it confuses its dreams with reality, just as the dreams we have while sleeping are real to us while we're dreaming them. Our version of reality is simply another type of dream. We create it, we manufacture it. Our experience of the world around us is our creation entirely; we are totally responsible for it.

Thus when we see "wrongness" we feel that something must be changed out there. How can we change an illusion through external means when it's totally an internal thing? As soon as we correct one "wrongness" more will spring up, but the sense of things being wrong can go on forever.

The images on the screen may be changing, but that is not the question; the question is whether the projector is still switched on. Until we've looked deeply into the nature of the mind itself, we go on and on altering the dream—but we are still dreaming.

Still another way of expressing mind's illusory version of reality is to say that the mind is always on drugs, it is always intoxicating itself. Mind is a drug addict. And what are its drugs? Its drugs are power, wealth, status, knowledge, prestige. Its drugs are food, sex, adventure, alcohol and pills. Its drugs are accomplishments, goals, saving the world, being infatuated, being part of a group, being creative. Its drugs are various beliefs and stories. Its drugs are hatred, anger, envy, pleasure, melancholy and so on.

Mind is always drugged, it can never see the real. Mind wants to be high so that it does not have to experience its suffering. But the nature of being high is that we must come down. And when mind comes down it immediately looks for another drug so that it can go up again. It wants a new man or woman, a new job, a new city, a new article of clothing, a new movie. And the process goes on, the mind never realizing that its drugs are not the solution.

Mind can never realize this because the mind lives in hope. Tomorrow will be better. But tomorrow never comes, never can come because when it arrives it is always today. The future cannot arrive. All that is ever here is the present moment. If we look closely we'll see that it is the very hope, the very desire itself that creates time.

Imagine sitting silently with no desires, blissful, calm. There is no time. We are simply in the eternal moment. Now let a single desire enter our being and we are in time again. If it will take a month to fulfill our desire then we have created the time of one month. If it will take an hour, then we have created the time of one hour.

And we have not one but thousands of desires large and small. Thus there is never enough time. We feel that time is slipping away from us, life is passing us by. That is why we are afraid of death, because we need more time. We have not yet fulfilled our desires, we have not yet accomplished what we want to do. We need more time and there is not enough of it. Our desires have created this. If we had no desires we would have no fear of death either; we would be ready for it.

Mind is in hell because of its desires. Have we noticed? When we're miserable time goes very slowly, it seems to drag on and on. Deep down, mind is always miserable since it spends its time outside the present moment. This is it, this is what hell looks like. It looks like our life when we're outside of the moment.

Conversely, if we had no desires, no goals, we would be totally blissful and time would have speeded up until there was no time—until there was just the moment. That would be paradise, heaven. But that is not possible for the mind, since it's filled with desires. Desire is its very essence.

 *Chapter Six*

When mind finally sees its own misery then it goes on a spiritual quest. Now instead of desiring money, power, possessions, pleasure, it desires God, heaven, enlightenment, transformation. Look deeply and we can see that nothing has changed. The goals may be different but the quality is the same; the mind is still seeking.

And it is this seeking which constitutes the very existence of the mind. Mind is motion, mind is occupation. And along with its spiritual quest mind usually becomes involved with metaphysical doctrines. And then it clings to them and disputes about them as if it's doing something important.

There is a great true story. A student of Zen said, "Master, do we survive death or not? Do we get reincarnated? And if so, do we retain our memory or lose it? Do we lose all aspects of our personality or are some aspects retained? And how long is it before we reincarnate?

"Or is this whole notion false and the Western notion of an immortal soul more accurate? And if so, do we retain our memory in heaven and hell or do we lose it? And are there other realms between here and heaven?"

"Your breakfast is getting cold," the master replied.

Mind can understand the complicated but has a hard time with the simple. Life is simple...a sunset, a rainstorm, a flower. Life is so simple that it is beyond our understanding. The mind cannot comprehend it, cannot comprehend simply being in the moment without any purpose or goal. So mind keeps trying to fit life into a box, to structure it, to create order out of what it sees as chaos. Mind feels deeply anxious when confronted with the unlimited and unknown, so it clings to its boxes and structures and tries desperately to be certain.

It asks questions. Why is there suffering? Why is there disease? Why is there hate? Why is there pain? Why is there death? Mind wants answers.

It doesn't see that the very impetus to ask questions and find answers arises from a feeling of discontent. When we are happy we don't ask why love exists. When we are healthy we don't ask why health exists. Only when there is suffering and dissatisfaction does questioning arise.

The mind is always in suffering since it is always trying to be somewhere else; thus it looks for answers. If it were in bliss, if it were simply in the moment all questions would drop from it. There would be no need. But mind cannot drop its grasping because it is the graspingness. The mind is diseased; only when there is illness is there a search for medicine.

Mind wants to impose an order on existence because existence is too wild, too chaotic. As Osho says, just when we're getting settled with our wisdom and our ways...we die. And a new baby is brought into the world, knowing nothing, not even knowing who it is.

It is a chaos! Big trees die and little seeds sprout. Galaxies die and new galaxies are born. A chaos! If mind had its way there would be no death, but then there would be no life either. Everything would be perfect, mechanical, efficient, ordered—and dead. Because the new would be impossible.

Chaos makes the new possible; that is its significance. Mind binds itself in rules, doctrines, attitudes, "shoulds," and then wonders why the flavor has gone out of life, why life seems more and more a matter of going through the motions. Mind becomes a prisoner of its own boxes.

Mind is a perfectionist, trying to find the structures and the answers that will be just right. It's an idealist, trying to attain some beckoning goal—political, moral, legal, cultural, scientific, artistic, economic, religious, whatever. And only the impossible looks really attractive as an ideal because only the impossible looks perfect.

And mind falls short of its ideal again and again...tries again, falls short again, becomes miserable again...the game goes on. It's an ego-trip, the impossible must be attained.

Only the possible and imperfect is human. Mind always desires the super-human, and the super-human is always inhuman. The most difficult thing for the mind is just to be ordinary, natural, "nothing special."

On the contrary, the ego/mind is trying very hard to be unique, special, extraordinary. It wants to stand out and be noticed. In fact this desire to be extraordinary is absolutely ordinary because it is ubiquitous, it's the everyday nature of the mind.

And mind is an extremist, going from one extreme to the other in its efforts to be unique and special. It can never be simply in balance because then it would cease to exist. Mind is the imbalance itself, and it will go to any lengths to be special. If it perceives failure in seeking pleasure then it will start seeking pain. If it thinks it can be superior by debasing itself it will do that. If it does not succeed in life then it will seek suicide, death.

Above all, mind is a doer. Something must be done—about one's life, about the world, about someone else, about this situation and that situation. And mind is innately violent, it is always willing to use force if necessary. To achieve its perfect ideal, coercion may have to be used. To the mind, the end justifies the means.

It wants to pry open the rosebud in order to obtain the rose, and is then surprised when petals fall to the ground and it holds nothing.

 *Chapter Seven*

So this is the mind: It feels separate and alone, and feels a need to survive. It sees much wrongness everywhere and wants to change things including parts of itself so that they will be "right." It is doingness, movement, struggle, striving—always trying to get somewhere but never being here. It's self-centered, selfish, always figuring its payoff in everything—even in altruism.

And what is its payoff? Survival of its attitudes, points of view, opinions, beliefs, rationalizations, acts, stories, presentations. The payoff is that it gets to be right. Finally, mind is a self-deceiver. It suffers but persuades itself it is reasonably happy. It lives in the past and future but persuades itself that it lives in the moment. It knows nothing but persuades itself that it knows the truth.

Now let's look deeper. The first thing to notice is that the mind is a crowd...at one moment satisfied, at another one sad, at one moment jealous, at another one frustrated, at one moment gratified, at another one bored. There is no unity. At different times a different actor has center stage. And so many thoughts!...pulling this way and that, on this subject and that, constantly changing.

If we consider emotions and sensations as simply different types of thought, then we notice that there is an endless parade of thoughts each different from the last. It is a melange, a grouping…a crowd.

The most interesting feature of a crowd is that there is no such thing as a crowd. Can we find a crowd apart from the individuals standing there? No. A crowd is an abstraction. Only individuals exist, but all of them standing together give the impression that something apart from the individuals exists. But only individuals exist.

Mind is like this. If we look closely we'll see that there is no such thing as mind. There are only individual thoughts. One thought following another in endless succession gives the feeling that something apart from thoughts themselves exists, but it doesn't. If we search for our mind we'll never find it. We'll only find individual thoughts. Mind is an abstraction. It doesn't actually exist.

What is this sense of "I" then, this sense of a separate existence? It is itself a series of thoughts, as the Buddha first pointed out. In fact, we think about ourself all the time. The telephone company did a study and found that by far the most common word used by people was "I." This "I" is actually an assumption, a conclusion formed out of a long succession of thoughts. It is itself a thought.

And if we look at our thoughts we'll see that they are things just like a glass or a chair. Each thought is like a wave rising out of the ocean. It appears out of nowhere, has a brief lifespan and then disappears back to where it came from.

Each thought rises and falls of its own accord, it is not under any control. Ask yourself: Can you change the thoughts you had yesterday? No. Can you change the thoughts that you will have tomorrow? No. Can you change the thought you're having right now? No. The "right now" has already passed. You'll be surprised—you can't change any of your thoughts. "You" have no control over them. They appear and disappear of their own accord. They are independent things.

This is the dilemma of the mind. It wants to control everything, and it imagines that it is the controller of its own decisions. It thinks of itself as the chooser, the decider, the self-guider. But actually it doesn't choose, it doesn't decide, it doesn't guide anything because it doesn't exist. All of its many choices and decisions are just more thoughts appearing of their own accord.

The irony is that the mind which spends its time struggling and striving to control things actually controls nothing at all because it doesn't exist. There is no self-guider, no chooser, no decider. Not that thoughts don't exist; they do. But there is no center guiding them all. There is no center at all, that's an illusion. Mind thinks of itself as the controller, the chooser, and that is exactly what is not there. Mind itself is not there.

Mind is terrified of not having control. It's terrified to be out of control because it conceives of itself as the controller. To be out of control is tantamount to being out of existence. At the deepest level, the mind cannot let go because it would be letting go of its own existence.

The paradox is that mind doesn't exist anyway, it only thinks it exists. It doesn't choose anything anyway; it only thinks it chooses. All that exists is isolated thoughts, one after another, some of which are that there is a self-guiding entity, that the entity makes decisions, that it knows the truth, that it is reasonably happy, and so on.

So we have the spectacle of something that does not actually exist spending its time trying to survive.

And this is not an academic matter. Because who or what is the mind? We are. All of our thoughts, emotions, attitudes, points of view, acts, stories, presentations and behavior patterns are all mind. We are the mind and the mind is us.

If we're imagining that there is some part of us which is separate from the mind, look again. There is no part of us that is not mind. Everything whatever that we conceive of ourself as being is simply mind.

 *Chapter Eight*

So to say that "mind" does not exist means that "you" and "I" do not exist. We think of ourselves as making decisions, but nobody is there to make them. "You" and "I" as self-guiders, as controllers, as choosers don't exist. There's nobody home. There are simply thoughts...and thoughts expressing themselves in activity through a servo-mechanism. Each thing that we think of as "us" is just another thought. There is no center. "You" and "I" are an illusion.

In fact, we're entirely a stimulus/response mechanism. A machine. A very complex machine, but a machine nevertheless. Normally we're accustomed to think only of objects such as jukeboxes and billiard balls as being completely in the realm of stimulus-response. We push a button on the jukebox and it plays "White Christmas." We knock a billiard ball and it rolls across the table.

But now let's move up the scale to plant life. A plant is a mechanism which is wired up to respond to the environment in a particular way. Light shines on it and its chemistry turns carbon and minerals to sugar and oxygen.

Now consider animals. Behaviorists demonstrate that animals act entirely within the parameters of stimulus-response. We may like that or not, approve of it or not, but the demonstration remains. It looks as if the cat chooses whether or not to walk into the bedroom, but actually it's simply responding to stimuli.

The difference between a plant and an animal in this respect is that an animal has a much more complex set of responses and it can distinguish between different types of stimuli. For instance, a pet can normally distinguish between someone it knows and someone it doesn't know, and it can respond accordingly in a variety of different ways. Stimulus-response in animals is much richer than that of plants, but the quality is the same.

Now let's move up to humans. A human being is also a stimulus-response mechanism, but a vastly more complex one. The human mechanism has an ability to distinguish between many thousands of different types of stimuli, and its range of responses is exceedingly broad and rich.

But this is perhaps not the most significant difference between the human and animal mechanisms. Perhaps the most significant difference is that we humans have a sound-track—an accompanying voice-over which takes all of our responses and explains them, justifies them, rationalizes them. This mental soundtrack is absolutely part-and-parcel of the stimulus-response system, but it gives rise to the idea of the "I" and thus to the idea that this "I" is guiding itself, that this "I" is choosing and deciding.

If a billiard ball is thrown off of a cliff it will fall. If an animal is thrown off a cliff it will fall and its organism will produce the emotion of fear on the way down. If you or I are thrown off a cliff we will fall and our responses will include a range of emotions such as fear, anger, regret, etc. However, in addition there will be something else—there will be a sound-track all the way down giving our stories as to why we were thrown, what's happening, what's going to happen and so on. All of which will be part of the response mechanism.

One of the things which makes it so difficult to see us humans as being entirely stimulus-response is that part of the mechanism's range of responses is the ability to alter its future responses to stimuli. One of our human responses is to alter our future responses. This very sophisticated response tends to look like "choice," even though it is still stimulus-response.

Another smokescreen is that the human mechanism's responses are often unpredictable—simply because we are so complex. The human mechanism is so unbelievably complex that there is often no way to predict what the responses will be, and this unpredictability is taken as further evidence of choice and control.

To say on the one hand that the mind is totally a stimulus-response mechanism and to say on the other hand that the mind creates its own version of reality seems like a paradox. But look closely and we'll see that the two statements are actually saying the same thing.

The mind responds to stimuli from the environment and part of its response is to label, categorize, judge, evaluate. On the basis of this it desires certain things and desires to avoid other things. And then it feels a sense of pleasure or pain depending on whether the environment provides what it desires. But what it desires, and its response to what it gets, is entirely a function of its own programming. Thus its sense of pleasure or pain in a given moment is dependent on its own stimulus-response conditioning, not on what the environment is providing.

In other words, mind responds to reality by creating its own version of reality. That horse is really no good. Cherries really taste better than melons. I was really justified in doing that. And so forth. Each of those statements is a version of reality; each is totally created by the mind.

Mind is totally stimulus-response and simultaneously it is totally responsible for its experience of reality. And not only is the mind stimulus-response, but the environment is too; it is all stimulus-response. Mind is trying to maintain control when there is no such thing as independent control. All parts of the environment, including the mind as one of those parts, are simply responding. Long before the days of behaviorists, the Buddha called this "co-dependent co-origination."

 *Chapter Nine*

Another way of considering this is to look at the mind as a very sophisticated computer. What are the components of a computer? A computer has input terminals where data comes in to be processed. It has output terminals where processed data is exported out to the environment. It has a central processing unit or CPU where the data is processed. And memory units where data and programs are stored.

And what is a program? A program is simply a list of instructions for the CPU to execute...first do this, then do that, then do this...on and on. Each instruction is simple, but since computers can do many millions of these instructions per second the end result can look and be very sophisticated indeed.

Now among a computer's programs is a master program—a list of instructions as to which programs will be done and in what order and under what circumstances. It is worth noting that the master program is a program just like any other program. It has no quality of self-determination or self-guidance about it. Depending on circumstances—stimuli—it responds according to its instructions. The result can be very refined, but is pure stimulus-response.

Now compare the mind to this computer. The mind's input is the five senses. Its output is thoughts, emotions, facial expressions, postures, actions, etc...our whole presentation, internally and externally. We can call all of the output by the word "tapes." A stimulus comes in and the mind processes it and comes up with a response, a tape. The tape may be anger, may be a smile, may be a thought about the weather, may be driving to work. Anything at all that the mind does, mental or physical, is a tape.

The mind has memory banks, of course, where data and programs of various kinds are stored. And the mind has an executive sub-routine which determines—on the basis of the directions in it—which program will be running at any given time and thus which tape will be presented.

This master program is about one thing and one thing only—survival. Each moment the executive sub-routine gives center stage to that subsidiary program which, according to its instructions, will most ensure survival. Survival may look like lying out on the beach getting a tan, it may look like finishing one's homework, it may look like getting jealous. The tape will be whatever seems to optimize survival the most in that moment, considering all factors.

And this business of survival can take strange forms. Let's say somebody slaps us in the face. The mind will search its memory banks for an earlier situation that looks similar. Let's say it finds an early episode where someone hit us and we went unconscious—but we survived. It pulls that program out of storage and runs it.

Now, in the present, after the slap we faint. To this mind, this is what looks most like survival. To some other mind with a different history, survival in that situation could take some other form—anger, propitiation, tears, whatever. But to this mind in this circumstance, survival looks most like fainting. So that is what it does.

But the mind goes further than that. Not only will it respond to this particular circumstance by fainting, but it will tend to set up situations over and over again where we get to faint and go unconscious. After all, we survive when we faint, don't we? So this mind will try to create circumstances where we can faint.

If we observe ourselves, we can see us creating certain patterns over and over again in our lives. The boss who always finds himself with irresponsible employees. The man or woman who is always late because of unavoidable circumstances. The person who always likes his new job until he gradually discovers that his co-workers are unfair to him. The number of possible patterns is infinite.

Mind gets a payoff from setting up such situations over and over; it gets to survive, it gets to be right about its point of view. Employees really are irresponsible. The circumstances really forced me to be late. My co-workers really are unfair. To the mind, this is survival. And it is all stimulus-response, it is all automatic machinery.

To see the mind as a computer (in its current beginning incarnation) conveys a sense of the mind's mechanicalness and automaticity, but it doesn't do it justice. For the mind is far more refined than any present-day computer. For example, as said before, part of the mind's programming is an ability to alter its response to future stimuli.

This quality is not unique to the mind, but is possessed by it to a unique degree here on earth at the present time. It's a very complex form of stimulus-response. These programming alterations are labeled as "improvements" when they are conscious and are taken by the mind as evidence of its self-choosing and independent nature.

And that's a really interesting feature of this computer, this mind. Part of its programming is the idea that it is self-guiding, that it is an "I," that it is an independent entity which controls itself and chooses among alternatives. And it's all illusion. There is no controlling, there is no choosing going on. There is no center, no "I." There is only stimulus-response, automatic programming.

If we were to dismantle this computer-mind we would never find this "I," we would never find this self-choosing essence because it is not there. It's no different in principle from dismantling a car. If we take all the parts away from a car there is nothing left; there is no essence of "car" apart from the parts. Similarly, if we were to take all automatic programming away from the mind there would be no mind left, no "I" left. Because it's not really there.

 *Chapter Ten*

Yet because of this sense of an "I," all sorts of bizarre phenomena take place. Since there is an "I," an attempt must be made to have this "I" survive. This separate "I" which does not actually exist tries to find ways to maintain its existence. This controller which in fact controls nothing tries to find ways to maintain and increase its control. No wonder the mind is so busy; it has an impossible problem to solve!

Actually the only problem is the "I" itself, but the mind cannot see this. Mind itself is the only problem, which is why the mind cannot solve its problem.

And so the whole game arises. The mind engages in its struggles and strivings, its activities and efforts in the attempt to solve a problem which cannot be solved. Preoccupied with the problem of survival and security, reaching toward the future and responding from the past, it can never be herenow. It can never let go, can never be completely in the moment because it ceases to exist if it does.

The mind collects power, money, status, allies, lovers, possessions, answers and agreement from the environment in the vain attempt to solve its problem. It projects its stories onto reality so that it doesn't see reality, and then ponders how reality ought to be changed. Mind tries to improve, change, get better and be different, but at bottom the game remains the same.

Just see deeply into the illusion. Mind is activity, mind is thought. Mind is the solving of problems, the running of tapes, the striving toward goals. It is all movement. Mind is occupation; occupation is mind. Since mind itself is the only problem in life, this means that the movement of the mind is the actual problem.

Further, since movement is mind, any movement or doingness at all will be contributing to the problem instead of solving it. Indeed, it is the movement or doingness which is the problem.

If we look closely we'll see that ultimately all of our attempts to improve, change, be different or better are part of the problem. Who is trying to be better? The mind. Trying to be better or different is simply a way of sustaining the mind's motion and thus of sustaining mind itself.

In attempting to change or be different, who is doing the attempting? The mind. The very effort involved is the problem, is the mind. It perpetuates the only suffering in life, which is wanting things to be different than they are at this moment.

That is, everything in our life which we conceive of as the solution to our problems is the problem. Every effort we make to achieve happiness is what keeps us in suffering deep down. Everything we do to make things better is what keeps things the way they are.

Watch. You'll see that the motions of the mind—its desires, discriminations, efforting, struggling—are the only problem. There is no problem outside of that.

The mind creates its own version of reality, which it then takes for reality itself. Finding this "reality" inadequate, it then attempts to change things, not seeing that the problem is not reality but its own created version of it. Reality is never a problem; only our stories about it are the problem.

The mind creates problems out of what is in order to give itself something to do, since the very doingness sustains the existence of the mind. There is no problem other than this craving of the mind itself.

If mind is the problem, then why not do something to nullify or alter or extinguish the mind? Just see that the very question comes from the mind. In attempting to extinguish the mind, who would be making the attempt? The mind. In endeavoring to alter the mind, who would be making the endeavor? The mind.

This is what the mind is doing now. It's trying to improve, change, make things different and better. All of that may temporarily palliate the problem, distract us from it or better adjust us to it, but it won't remove or solve it. How can it? All of that is the problem.

Our desire to have things be something other than what they are, as Byron Katie says, is the suffering in our life. All desire is wanting something that isn't herenow. The desire itself is the suffering because it prevents us from experiencing the perfection and enoughness of this moment.

Thus, our desires to reach satisfaction in life are what keep it unsatisfactory. Our desires to alter the world so that it will be more acceptable are what keep it unacceptable in our version of reality. Our desires to make things perfect are what keep them imperfect.

It is possible to deeply see that nothing can be done. There's nothing we can do to solve the situation or escape from it, because anything we do becomes simply another way of maintaining it.

There is no way to get out of the mind because "we" are the mind, there is no part of what we think we are which is left out. The very idea that "you" exist (as a separate entity) is the problem of life; how therefore are "you" going to solve the problem?

 *Chapter Eleven*

So, you may ask, why not just let go then? Why not just accept everything the way it is? Observe. This is simply another way for the mind to preserve itself. For who is deciding to let go? Who is deciding to accept everything? The mind. How can the controller not try to control? How can the achiever not try to achieve? How can the improver not try to improve? It's like asking the nose not to be the nose.

The mind can't really let go or accept what is, because the very attempt to do so perpetuates the mind, perpetuates the non-accepter. Of course we can pretend to be accepting, we can convince ourself that we are accepting everything, but that's just a head-trip. Deep down the solidity of the "I" is being reinforced.

What about other solutions then? To love everyone. To serve others. To seek God or enlightenment. Or to not give a damn. But look deeply. To decide to love everyone is just another tape. Who is it that is deciding to love? The mind. And deciding to or trying to love is a misguided effort because real love has nothing to do with trying to be loving.

Love just happens; it's effortless and involuntary. It's a falling; it just happens of itself. There's no way to force it.

Attempting to love is of the mind. It's false and far removed from love itself.

Well then, perhaps we'll decide to forget about ourself and serve others. But how can we truly serve others when we can't serve ourself? If the water in our own pond is still muddy, how can we expect to clear up the muddiness in the ponds of others? What looks good to us may have a bad result. To think we are doing something good is of the mind; it reinforces the illusions that constitute the mind.

Not that serving others is bad. But when it truly happens it's like love—involuntary, effortless. And there is no thought that one is serving others, no decision about it. It just happens.

Perhaps, then, we'll seek God or enlightenment. But who will be doing the seeking? Yes, the mind. To seek God or enlightenment or transformation or whatever is just another way for the mind to sustain itself, another way for the mind to keep up its motion.

Seeking money-power-pleasure and seeking the divine may look much different, but they have the same quality. It's still a seeking. It's still an attempt to get to someplace other than where we are. It's still the mind trying to go beyond the mind. The trying is the mind. The solution is the obstacle.

A joke: How can we find God? She is waiting at home for us, and meanwhile we cannot find Her because we are off seeking Her.

Then there is the ultimate solution—to just not give a damn, to simply not do anything at all about it. But that does not alter anything, because the deep-down suffering is still there. And who is it that is choosing not to give a damn? Yes, the mind. To choose not to care is to perpetuate the chooser, is to perpetuate this illusory "I." It's the same game and the problem continues. Pretending that it doesn't exist is merely another way for the problem to sustain itself.

Mind is the problem, but look carefully and we see that there is nothing we can do to escape from it. Because all escape attempts are the mind, are the problem. Even deciding not to escape is another attempt to escape because such a decision perpetuates the illusion that there is a decider. All attempts to get there are ways of not getting there. All ways out lead back in. It is like holding up a mirror to a mirror—an infinite regression, limitless, never-ending.

Everything whatsoever is grist for the mind in terms of it perpetuating itself. There is absolutely no activity of any kind that cannot serve the mind's purpose, since activity is the mind. All efforts to choose, to struggle, to seek goals and to control are mind. Conversely, all efforts not to choose, not to struggle, not to seek goals and not to control are also mind. It's all mind.

All thoughts, feelings, attitudes, opinions, sensations, viewpoints, acts, positions, stories, presentations, responses— all of it, everything sustains the mind, is the mind. Nothing is left out. Everything whatsoever about us is part-and-parcel of the problem. "We" ourselves are the problem.

If "you" and "I" are the problem in our life, how can that problem be solved? It can't. How can we get away from this ficticious "you" and "I" then? We can't; that's who "we" are. How can we improve our situation then? We can't. We can fool ourselves of course, but at the deepest level there is no way to improve it.

Just see that all our solutions are the problem, all our escapes are the imprisonment, all of our getting better is the illness. Further, see that we must try to solve it, escape from it, improve it because that is the nature of the mind, that is what it does, that is who "we" are. It is totally unsolvable. All of our solutions and non-solutions are the obstacle.

Question: If all this is so, then what should be done? Answer: Nothing, because nothing can be done. Question: If nothing can be done, then where do we go from here? Answer: Nowhere. Question: But then what is the point of all this? Answer: There is no point.

The mind thinks that everything must have a point, because otherwise what is the point? This, too, is part of the problem. The mind thinks that these words must have a point, but actually they have no point. These words are just concepts, structures, boxes—of no importance.

Thus there's nothing "true" about any of this. None of the concepts being used here are true in any sense. Useful temporarily, perhaps, but not true. If the mind clings to them that is simply another way of perpetuating itself, perpetuating the separate "you" and "me."

In fact, a logician would note that these concepts have contained a number of contradictions. It doesn't matter. There will be more; it has to be that way. Besides, they're fun.

All these words—past and future and this sentence too—are just devices to create a situation where something other than concepts can happen. That may not happen immediately, it may not happen for months or years, but it doesn't matter because it can't be rushed or forced anyway. And it can't be slowed down either.

In truth—do you enjoy the joke?—in truth, these words are merely a playing in the sandbox, a passing of toys back and forth, a building of castles in the damp sand. There is no point to them at all. See the point.

Existence

 *Chapter Twelve*

The central dilemma that we humans find ourselves in, the central problem of our life, is not solvable at the level at which the problem is posed. It is an extraordinary problem in that all the attempts to solve it constitute the problem itself. Every attempt to change it, improve it, suppress it, solve it—only deepens it. It is like someone in quicksand whose every effort to get out only sinks him deeper and deeper into the sand.

What is the problem? The problem is that the mind is a problem-solving mechanism which is obsessed by the problem of its own survival. It seems as if this problem is something inherited by the mind. It seems as if the mind finds itself alone and separate in a world which seems indifferent at best and overtly hostile at worst. But it isn't that way. The mind creates its own problem—and then spends its energy trying to solve its self-created problem.

Of course, since the problem is an illusion it cannot be solved. The mind as controller, chooser, guider of its destiny does not exist—only stimulus-response exists. If the mind-as-controller doesn't exist, how can it survive? By pretense; by not seeing that it doesn't exist.

The mind is a magic show, a trick with mirrors, it's the magician who makes something appear to be so when it isn't. You see the lady in the box sawed in half, yet she is not sawed in half; something is ficticious. This is like the mind. The non-existent mind-magician survives through the sleight-of-hand of working on the problem of its survival.

If we look at our life carefully, we see that it is about survival. The mind survives through the problem itself; the attempts to solve the problem are the mind. If the striving of the mind were to vanish, the mind itself would vanish.

The mind is willing to spend an entire lifetime trying to keep this shell game going—trying to arrange things so that something which doesn't exist can survive. It's willing to use a whole lifetime in the misery of this absurd struggle.

And it is not only willing to do so but it must do so; that is its nature. The mind—you and I—will act out this comic tragedy right up to the moment of stepping into our grave. The mind has no choice; this is what it must do. It cannot do anything else than be the magician—and it is the ultimate magician, for its trick is that the magician herself appears to be there but is non-existent.

So the problem cannot in any way be solved, since all efforts to do so constitute the problem. The problem can only be transcended, but that transcendence is not a doingness of any kind. Nothing is done. Nothing is improved or changed, since at the deepest level no improvement or change is possible. Rather an awareness, a seeing arises and then the problem is no longer experienced as a problem.

Since it is no longer experienced as a problem, the problem can be said to have disappeared. Nothing has changed, the situation remains the same, but the problem has vanished.

In fact there is not now and there has never been any problem in life—other than the magic-show, the mind's interpretations and stories about what's happening.

To actually see this is to have transcended the problem of mind. And when that happens the problem of life becomes like the favorite toy of a child when the child has grown up— it's simply left behind. The toy is still there in the closet and nothing has changed about it. But now it's no longer relevant. It has been transcended.

This transcendence, of course, is not a doingness of any kind. It's nothing that the mind does, nothing that "you" and "I" do. Transcendence is not accomplished by the mind at all. Rather, it is the mind itself that is transcended. "You" and "I" are transcended.

But how in the world is this done? Because remember, there is no way out for the mind, no way out for "you" and "I." All of our attempts to change our life in any way merely keep it fundamentally the way it is. So how does this transcendence arise?

Consider the following: Imagine a caterpillar which creates a goal of becoming a butterfly. It spends its time imagining ways to do so, trying this method and that method, but nothing seems to work. Because no matter how hard it tries to be a butterfly, it still stays a caterpillar.

It may be an "improved" or "better" caterpillar but its fundamental essence is still caterpillarness.

Now imagine for a moment that our caterpillar could think. If it could, it could not actually even conceive of being a butterfly because its only experience is of being a caterpillar. So if it thinks of becoming a butterfly it's actually thinking of being a better caterpillar.

Being a butterfly is literally unthinkable. Therefore our caterpillar's attempts to become a butterfly are manifested as attempts to improve itself as a caterpillar. Futile. How *does* our caterpillar become a butterfly?

The thing to notice is that nothing the caterpillar does causes it to transmute into a butterfly. Nature handles the problem, the caterpillar doesn't have to. All it has to do is be a caterpillar—which it already is—and the transmutation then *happens by itself.*

The key is *being* a caterpillar. If the caterpillar is busy trying to become a butterfly or a better caterpillar it is not simply being a caterpillar. Let it just be a caterpillar—then the butterfly part will take care of itself.

 *Chapter Thirteen*

In the case of a caterpillar that's no problem because a caterpillar has no mind, it has no notion of itself as a chooser or self-guider. But in our case what will we do? We are the mind, everything we've ever thought of ourselves as being is the mind. If the mind decides to "be the way it is," that is just another decision by the mind, it's the mind surviving. And the mind can never be herenow, can never simply be the way it is. No, it's very busy trying to get somewhere. So how is this paradox resolved?

To answer that question we must introduce the notion of being or the true self. It is who we really are, but it is not "you" or "I." It has nothing to do with who or what we think we are. It has nothing to do with the mind, nothing to do with our tapes, models, programs, voice-overs, thoughts, emotions, sensations, stories, actions, presentations, metaphysics or anything else about "you" or "I." No, it's who we really are. And it's beyond the world of stimulus-response.

The true self is like an empty blue sky—vast, silent, unchanging. It's pure consciousness, pure existence. It has no form, and it doesn't look like anything. It is reality, but has nothing to do with the mind's stories of reality.

It is truth, but has nothing to do with concepts or words. It is beauty itself, but a beauty beyond form or image. It is bliss, but it has nothing to do with what is normally thought of as happiness because it has no cause. It is peace, stillness, silence, but it has nothing to do with what normally is thought of as relaxation in human life.

No formulations of any kind can really describe being, the self, the existence. It is emptiness, nothing, the absence of anything. It is unsayable, unthinkable, not reachable by any conceptualization. That is, we can conceptualize it but the conceptualization is just nonsense because it has nothing to do with existence or being itself. Being is unlimited and words are limited—the gap is more or less unbridgeable. Thus all words and concepts about it are fundamentally false, because words come from a context of exclusion and existence is not that way.

Let's look directly. In order for any conceptualization at all to be formed something must be excluded; otherwise we have the totality, the whole, but no concept. In order to form the concept of "pencil" we must exclude that which is "not-pencil." In order to form the concept of "red" we must exclude that which is "not-red." This is why no mental formulation, no conceptual system no matter how subtle or sublime can be the truth. Because concepts are ultimately grounded in limitation, exclusion, logic—and truth is unlimited, non-exclusive and, to the mind, illogical.

What is truth? Truth is a sunset, truth is rain on the streets, truth is percolating coffee. It is whole. Truth is like a hologram in that each part of it contains the totality. Truth is not a sum of the parts and no amount of explanation can ever reach it; it simply is what it is.

What is truth? Truth is a rose—not the word "rose" nor any theory about roses but purely a rose itself. We can experience a rose, we can experience reality, we can experience truth, but as soon as we try to put it into words we distort it. We could write a million words about experiencing a rose on a warm spring evening but they would not even come close to the experience itself.

To really see this is to understand, as Osho often said, that ignorance is so vast that it can never be destroyed. What is water? Science answers that it is H_2O, hydrogen and oxygen. What is hydrogen, what is oxygen? Science answers that they are certain configurations of protons and electrons, matter and energy, but these are just new names.

Nobody knows what an electron is, nobody knows what matter is, nobody knows what hydrogen is and nobody knows what water is. We have added a few new labels and categories, but the mystery is still profound, totally impenetrable. Our ignorance is infinite, it can never be overcome. It is not possible to ever really know anything.

This being so, it follows that even the simplest things are basically incommunicable, they can't actually be accurately talked about. Words immediately distort them. If this is true of water or a rose, how much more true is it of words about being...self...existence. The moment we talk about it we fall into error and distortion and falsity.

63

Thus when we say that being is truth or bliss or peace it must be remembered that this is the language of poetry, of metaphor, of indirect allusion. Even the very words "being" or "self" or "existence" are merely labels created by the mind, and we do well not to take them literally.

The apt phrase used in the Buddhist Surangama Sutra is that all words and concepts about existence are "a finger pointing at the moon." Words can only indicate, suggest; they are not the moon—reality—but only a finger pointing at it.

The mind, however, misses the moon and focuses on the finger. Mind pores over philosophies, theologies, metaphysical systems and then feels that the existence is really such-and-such a way. Mind always misses the point. Even the concepts in this paragraph are just toys in the sandbox.

An interesting true story: A seeker once came to the Zen master Joshu and asked, "What is the Buddha? Who is the Buddha? Where can he be found?" Joshu replied, "Go into the temple. You will find the Buddha there." Then the man said, "But inside the temple there is only a stone statue. And you know and I know that a stone statue is not the Buddha." Joshu replied, "You are absolutely right. A stone statue is not the Buddha."

And so the man said, "Then who is the Buddha?" And Joshu replied, "Go into the temple. You will find the Buddha there."

A curious story. This seeker had seen beyond the symbolism of stone statues, but not beyond other symbolisms. So he assumed that Joshu was talking about external temples.

But Joshu had no interest in external temples, he was talking about the temple within. He was saying that unless we see into the nature of the mind we are lost, we'll never find out that we're already the Buddha.

Mind needs excitement; it needs diversion, the chase, the search. It is like a spider constantly spinning and then being caught in its own web. The spinning, the excitement, the activity, the seeking are smokescreens which prevent us from seeing into the nature of all this. We've become like a man searching around the world for the nose on his face. So he can't see that he already has what he's looking for.

Truth is the immediate, the foreground, but we don't see it because we're scanning the heavens for it.

Chapter Fourteen

Mind is enmeshed in symbolism, in stories, and it takes these for reality, for truth. Yet nothing which can be expressed in words or symbols is "true"; neither is it "false." Rather, it is merely useful or non-useful. Science is replete with examples of "truths" which became supplanted. First light was a particle, then a wave; now it's something of both. First the world was flat, now it is round; someday it may be perceived in some other way. First Newton's laws were "true"; now relativity is considered "true," and someday it in turn will be supplanted. No concept or law or symbolic relation is ultimately "true"; it's simply useful or not useful for a limited period.

Is "The tree is green" true? Certain vibrations are hitting our eyes and we have agreed to label those "green." A different interpretation of the vibrations we have agreed to label "tree." When we say "The tree is green" we're simply attaching two labels together; it may be useful, but there's nothing true about it. Conjoining the labels "tree" and "green" has a lot of agreement, but somebody may disagree—to them the tree may be chartreuse.

This might seem like an out-of-the-way or irrelevant matter, but it extends into our whole life.

Let's say we feel that our girlfriend is boring. To us that's true, but to someone else it's false. Let's say we feel we don't have enough money. To us that's true—our desires outstrip what we have. But actually it's a matter of desires—the mind—rather than money. We're creating our experience of the sum of money we have.

Similarly, we're creating our experience of everything whatsoever in our life. It's all our creation. We create what is good, bad, true, false, right, wrong, desirable and undesirable in our life.

Existence is none of these categories. It simply is what it is. It is pristine, pure, ever-new. It has no past, no future, it is simply herenow. Then the mind comes in and imposes its tapes and stories upon it. The mind imposes its judgments, evaluations, discriminations, dualities, categories, labels and multiplicities. It boxes up reality and then is caught in its own box. It projects its own movie onto the screen of reality and then lives in the movie. And it's in deep suffering because it's off in the past or the future somewhere.

Something is wrong, because happiness is the criterion in life. If our path in life is giving us deep bliss, deep abiding joy then it is the right path. But look carefully and let's ask ourselves truthfully: How many moments in our life have we experienced such profound rapture and peace that we had no desire for anything more whatsoever? A handful of times?

If bliss is the criterion—and it is—then we're missing the mark. What is wrong? We go on fixing things, improving, solving problems—and our situation remains the same.

Seeing this, we begin to look at the root of the problem—the mind itself—instead of the leaves. Once we begin to see directly into the con game of the mind we're astonished, stupefied as to why we go on carrying this madman.

For it is us as the self, existence itself, who is carrying the mind. Not the self that we identify with—our thoughts, emotions, attitudes, points of view, etc.—for that is all mind. No, us as existence itself is carrying it.

Let's be alert now, for the mind will immediately try to box up "the self," "the existence." Mind will create pictures of what it is, images of what it looks like: Infinite space. White light. Blue light. Darkness. Pure energy. The eternal. And so on. None of these are wrong, and neither are they right. None of these symbols can be taken seriously, for they're all just playthings. They're only fingers pointing at the moon.

And there are many such symbols, reflecting the attempts of those who have awakened to communicate the incommunicable.

There is the tradition known as the *via positiva*, the positive way, in which existence is given some of the labels we have been using, such as being, the self, reality, the whole, the eternal, the infinite, consciousness, truth. These are not separate aspects of the existence but merely different labels for the same thing. Yet because these positive labels use a descriptive form they are deceiving, they tend to be taken literally.

To get around this tendency some other traditions have followed the *via negativa*, the negative way, in referring to existence. They refer to it by indicating what it is not.

Thus in the Upanishads there's a famous passage which describes the existence as "not this, not that." Whatever description we use, it is not that. This seems a bit closer. For referring to the existence is akin to describing the color blue to someone born blind: Is it loud? No. Is it soft? No. Is it rough? No. Is it smooth? No. Is it sweet? No. Is it fragrant? No. Is it melodic? No. Saying what it is not is in a sense more accurate than trying to say what it is.

So when the existence is referred to in these traditions it's given names such as nothingness, emptiness, the void, the abyss. The advantage of such labels is that they don't suggest any particular attribute to which the mind can cling, since all attributes are negated. On the other hand, the mind can take even "nothingness" or "emptiness" literally—so it's fruitful to remember that even via negativa labels are not actually true or accurate.

Still another way of approaching being or existence is to refer to it as oneness or the non-dual or the One. When mind looks upon the world it looks through its glasses of discrimination and sees a multiplicity of separate entities—including itself—all struggling for survival. This, however, is just the appearance.

Beneath the surface, existence is a totality; it is One. At this level there is no struggle of any kind because there must be a duality in order for struggle to exist; struggle must be for something or against something. But the One is everything; it excludes nothing, desires nothing, seeks nothing, is against nothing. How then can there be a struggle? The existence is playing, it likes to look upon itself from different points of view...different entities. And part of this play or *lela* is that those points of view which have consciousness imagine themselves to be separate entities.

 *Chapter Fifteen*

Picture an ocean...waves moving on its surface. Each wave rises up, exists for a while, then falls back into the ocean from whence it came. Now imagine that each wave has the notion that it exists separately. Naturally, each wave is then concerned with survival, with the problem of how to go on existing.

Notice that the problem is unsolvable, because in fact at some point the wave is going to cease to exist. But this is only a problem at the level of wave, where the wave is trying to go on existing separately. The wave is clinging to its separateness, which creates its problem. Notice that at the level of ocean there is no problem, because the ocean is neither coming into existence nor going out of existence. Nor is it trying to survive. It simply is.

Notice too that at no time is the wave actually separate from the ocean. Indeed, even to call it a "wave" separates it in our minds, but in fact there is only the ocean. Even if the wave thinks it is separate, it is not. The attempt to survive perpetuates its sense of separateness, but actually it is never separate. There is only the ocean, evolving and changing its form on the surface, yet remaining always the same.

Actually, the only problem the wave has is that it is trying to solve a problem. The moment it gives up its problem of survival it is at the level of ocean, where there is no problem of any kind. At that level there is only the serenity and bliss of existence itself.

The wave is already the ocean; it doesn't have to achieve anything in order to become the ocean. It already *is* that. Its only problem is its illusion that it has to achieve something, that it has to get somewhere, that it has to make its way, that it has to survive. The shift from the level of wave to the level of ocean can come in an instant; it takes no time because nothing has to be changed or achieved. Everything is already in place except for the wave dropping its cherished illusion of being separate.

But notice that the wave itself cannot drop this illusion of separateness. Separateness is how it conceives of its existence; how can it drop itself? Similarly, the mind feels separate and will always feel separate; that is its nature. Separateness is its very existence; it cannot see through itself.

But if the mind somehow disappears then there is no problem. Then Being, Existence shines forth from that empty vessel, It experiences itself without any impediment from the mind. It was always there. When the mind is gone, Being is. It is there automatically since it was never not there.

An analogy can be used of a lamp encased in mud. The light is there but it cannot be seen, cannot be experienced because of the mud blocking it. Remove that mud, and the light that was always there is revealed.

Another analogy is of the sun shining on a cloudy day. If clouds cover the sky then the sun cannot be seen, yet it is still there. This is our situation. Those clouds are thoughts, stories, tapes. Let one cloud be removed and the sun can be seen a little. Let another be removed and the sun can be seen a little more.

The sun is then seen through the gaps, just as Being or Existence is experienced through gaps in the thoughts/tapes of the mind. As more gaps open up and the Mystery is more available, it can be said—in a manner of speaking—that the Self awakens. But the mind itself cannot open up the gaps, as any attempt to do so would be just another tape, just another cloud in the way.

To say that Being or the Self awakens is perhaps to give the impression that there is a separate being or self in each person. But no, only minds are separate; that is why they're an illusion. Being is always One. Putting it another way, my true self and your true self are the same self. There is only one Self, one Being, one Existence, one Ocean. In the Upanishads it is said that Atman is Brahman—the individual soul is the Existence, is the totality. There is only the One.

This is keenly disappointing to the mind, which hopes to survive physical death through the notion of an individual soul or essence which goes to heaven or reincarnates into a new body or whatever. But heaven and hell and anything we could desire in the afterlife are all here now. "The kingdom of heaven is within you," Jesus said. It is Existence itself which reincarnates into new forms.

Existence keeps taking new forms and the surface of things keeps changing just as the surface of the ocean is constantly in motion. But underneath, all is changeless, silent, still. Who we really are is vast and open like the sky. Who we really are cannot die because it was never born.

All aspects of the mind, on the other hand, are merely surface and are destined for annihilation. All the things that we think we are, all of the things which we cling to—our attitudes, emotions, thoughts, memories, patterns, viewpoints—will die as surely as a blooming rose or a wave on the ocean.

All of what we think is important and unique about us is transitory and will fade as quickly as a leaf in autumn. The mind's problem is not solvable. It is trying to survive and it cannot. And meanwhile its efforts and struggles keep it in anguish, which it polishes over with transitory gratifications. This going-through-the-motions, this daily round—eating, sleeping, working, relaxing, improving, eating, sleeping, all as a means to an end—is what we call life.

So the problem of life can only be transcended. It can never be solved. All of the mind's efforts to solve it, improve it, change it, make it better only deepen the problem. Yet the problem can be transcended. What happens is that Being awakens from a dream, so to speak, and discovers It's the Ocean and not the wave. The problem in the dream does not need to be solved. Awakening is enough. Then the dream vanishes and the unsolvable problem vanishes with it.

 *Chapter Sixteen*

But how is this awakening, this transcendence accomplished? If the mind does not do it, if indeed there is no doing involved, then how does it happen? To answer this question, let us look at the mind from still another perspective:

At each moment the mind is running its stimulus-response programs—tapes, thoughts, stories. These programs are used to paint reality, to project on the screen of Existence the version of reality that the mind wants to see. In order to see these tapes as reality it is necessary not to see them as tapes—that is, it is necessary not to notice them as generated within the mechanism. The tapes must be seen as being *out there;* they must be seen as the real world, as reality, as "the way things really are."

An analogy of watching a movie can be used. If we get really engrossed in watching the story on the screen we may forget that it's not real. We're feeling anxiety or hope, tears or joy, when suddenly the projector breaks down and the screen goes dark. And then we remember that it's only a movie, that it's not real.

Similarly, if with one of the mind's tapes or programs we suddenly remember that it's only a tape, if we suddenly notice it *as* a tape—a beautiful tape or an ugly tape, but still only a tape—then the movie is over for that moment. The program is exposed as merely a program; the screen has gone dark, so to speak.

In that moment we no longer see the tape as reality because we are seeing it as merely a tape, as merely a program. Since the purpose of a tape is to present itself as reality, the instant its lack of reality is exposed the program simply stops running. The tape disappears. The program, the tape, the act, the number, the thought—whatever we want to call it—just goes back to where it came from. In that instant of awareness there is no mind anymore; there is only Being.

Who or what does the noticing? The mind cannot do it because the mind is inescapably stuck in its dreams, in its manufactured version of reality. Only the Self, only the Being can be aware. It is awareness. The moment the Self notices that the particular tape running at that moment is simply a tape and not reality, the moment the Self notices the program *as* a program—in that moment the program that was running simply disappears. In that moment there is only the Self, there is no mind. Metaphorically speaking, in that moment the Self has awakened, the wave has discovered it is the Ocean.

But in the next moment another tape will be called up and run as a response to stimuli from the environment. In this metaphor, if the Self identifies with this tape and sees it as reality, then, so to speak, the Self is caught once more; then the Being has been sucked into the illusion once again. Again It has fallen asleep. Once more It has become identified with the mind, with the automatic stimulus-response mechanism. Now the survival programming of the mechanism is in the driver's seat.

Then at some point another moment comes when the Self notices a program *as* a program, notices a tape as simply a projected version of Reality itself. The tape vanishes; it can no longer present itself as real. In that instant the Self can be said to be awakened once more.

So it goes, back and forth. Self awakens from its long slumber for a moment, then goes back to sleep again. And again It awakens, only to return to sleep once more. In the beginning the Self awakens only fitfully. It is like someone engrossed in a vivid dream trying to remember that it is only a dream—and the moment she does, of course, the dream is no longer there. It is like someone in a deep hallucination trying to remember that the hallucination is not real.

In the beginning this process seems difficult because the moments of awareness are few and far between. But that is just the appearance. The moment of awareness itself is not difficult because awareness is not a doingness of any kind. The Self does not exist in time or space; it is not engaged in any activity, striving or effort. So awareness is not something that is done; it simply is. It simply happens.

If awareness of a tape is an effort then it is not awareness, it is something being done by the mind. For the mind is all about effort and struggle and striving; the mind can never be effortless since it is always in one way or another trying to be somewhere other than where it is.

Awareness, not being of the mind, is effortless. It takes place outside of the whole stimulus-response mechanism, and isn't an activity. It is not active, but passive.

The difference can be seen in a metaphor suggested by Osho. Imagine waiting in a train station where we are to meet our lover. We actively watch the doors; we are looking for a particular face, our lover's face. We are not interested in other faces. This is active awareness. This is mind. Mind is looking for a result; it is looking for something in particular.

Now imagine sitting by the side of a river in autumn, watching the leaves on the river float by. As each leaf passes by, it is noticed without effort. No leaf is more important than any other, yet no leaf passes by without being noticed. There is no concern for results, there is no end in view. There is just a choiceless, silent watching. This is passive awareness. This is awareness by the Self; indeed, it is the Self. Each leaf is simply noticed and let go; there is no concern about it.

This is what one does with one's tapes, programs, thoughts, feelings, sensations, models, acts and demands. We simply notice whatever comes up, whatever is running, with bare attention. Nothing is added; no judgment, no evaluation, no feeling that it's good or bad, or that it should or shouldn't be there.

We simply allow what is there to be there, and notice it without encouragement or condemnation. Adding encouragement, condemnation, judgment, evaluation, or anything else would be doing something with the tape/story, and pure awareness is a non-doingness.

78

We allow each leaf—each tape—to come into our awareness without desire or avoidance, and we allow it to leave without clinging or pushing. There are no preferences. Each thought is allowed to come in and it's allowed to go. It is simply noticed without adding anything. And if the mind does add something to it, then the addition is also simply noticed.

It's like noticing waves on the sea. Each wave comes up out of the depths, is noticed and allowed to be, and then disappears back into the ocean from which it came. It is like watching clouds in the sky. Each cloud appears, moves across the sky, then disappears. There is no reason for the cloud to be there; it just happens to be there. And while it is there it is silently watched. We watch the thoughts of the mind in just the way that we would watch clouds pass across the sky.

 *Chapter Seventeen*

Depending on the tradition this is called *awareness* or *witnessing* or *mindfulness*. Sometimes it is referred to as *bare attention* or *self-remembering*. The name doesn't matter, for the same phenomenon underlies the different names. It is a deep allowing. It's a deep let-go. It is a deep willingness for whatever exists to exist. It is a deep loving of whatever is there, and choosing it to be the way it is. It's a deep gratitude and celebration of what is. It's a deep observation of what exists without attachment or avoidance.

There are two main branches on this tree. The first is about beginning where we are—in our daily life. For instance, if we're taking a shower we're usually not herenow with it; we're not aware of the loveliness of the water falling on us. Instead, we're thinking of various things, wondering about this and that, getting ready for work or whatever. Usually, we're not just taking a shower when we're taking a shower.

Using awareness in daily life would mean, for instance, noticing the stories/tapes that are running as we're taking the shower. It would mean noticing what is getting in the way of just being there with the shower. As we notice the tapes, we neither reject them nor encourage them.

We do nothing with them. It's simply a noticing that they are tapes, that the mind is in motion. One accepts them, allows them, chooses them to be there, but not as an active thing. Rather, the acceptance is implicit in the awareness itself. As we notice the tapes as just tapes, the motion as just motion, the tapes become more flimsy—and then we're just taking a shower, nothing else.

When we see a story as reality instead of as a story, it's as if we've become fascinated by one of the leaves in the stream and are now following it as it moves downstream. Our attention is caught; we're clinging. Then we're living in the version of reality produced by taking that thought *as* reality. Then we miss reality itself by clinging to something limited. Conversely, as we simply watch each tape with detachment as it comes in and goes out, with no preferences, then we arrive at the doorway of the spiritual—the present moment.

When Buddha talks about attachment being the cause of suffering, an image can arise of attachment to objects or people. And indeed we do get attached to people and objects. But we do so because of the stories we tell ourselves.

We cannot be attached to people or objects without being attached to our story about them. That is the real attachment that the Buddha was talking about. And that clinging means seeing that belief or story as reality. If there is no "reality" in the perception of a tape/story then there will be no attachment to it either. Then it will be just another belief or story and will be seen as such. Divested of the quality of being "true" and "real," it ceases to engage us.

Thus attachment to a person or object actually consists of the moment-to-moment clinging that occurs when there is a story about it. And the interactions and circumstances of daily life tend to bring up exactly those tapes that most need to be noticed. So using mindfulness moment-to-moment in everyday situations is a fast way to bring awareness to deep-seated attachments.

But also, there is great value in sitting silently, free for a period of the hustling and bustling of the daily routine, so that one can observe without distraction the tapes that bubble up out of the depths of one's mind. In the silence of just sitting still, we can more easily become aware of the movement of the mind. Then, as the stories gradually become more flimsy, the mind also becomes more flimsy since the mind is nothing other than its stories. Then Reality starts to move through us a little more.

These two approaches complement each other well. It's helpful to use awareness in periods of silence as well as in one's daily routine. When used together they open a common door—the gradual disappearance of the mind.

In Zen they call this disappearance *no-mind*. In this state all dualities, all models, all beliefs, concepts, limitations, demands, exclusions, positions and versions of reality have been transcended, for there is no mind to sustain them. In the resulting emptiness, Existence can play its Melody through us more and more, like Breath through a hollow flute.

 *Chapter Eighteen*

When we look closely at the stories we give meaning to, the positions we get on, it becomes clear that certain stories or positions recur over and over. There are dominant themes or leitmotifs in the life of each of us, and it's no accident that each of us creates certain situations, runs certain tapes, gets on certain positions, again and again.

It's similar to a post-hypnotic suggestion. Let's suppose that someone hypnotizes us and implants a post-hypnotic suggestion that whenever he raises an eyebrow we will crave a bowl of soup, but that we won't remember the suggestion. Now after the hypnotic session we will feel perfectly normal. We and the hypnotist are talking, let's say, when suddenly he raises an eyebrow. Immediately we will desire a bowl of soup, and to justify this desire we will mention something perhaps about it being time for lunch.

Notice that the justification we use has nothing whatever to do with the impulse itself. Our desire for soup is because of the post-hypnotic suggestion. Yet on top of that we will add a soundtrack, a voice-over, a story or rationalization about why we are desiring soup now. That is, we'll justify our impulse. That's one of the things the mind does.

More than that, we'll feel that we've *chosen* now to have a bowl of soup because it's lunchtime, when in fact we're acting out a situation which is entirely mechanical for us, which is entirely stimulus-response. If we spend our life around people who often raise an eyebrow we will find ourself frequently desiring a bowl of soup. And in each case where we have a bowl of soup we'll feel that we have chosen to do so, that we've made a decision about it.

And in each case our mind will supply a reason as to why we've chosen to have a bowl of soup at that moment. And the reason in each case will be entirely irrelevant because our having a bowl of soup is pure stimulus-response—yet we will feel that we are the decider, the controller, the chooser in the situation.

It will become a dominant theme in our life. We'll become known as a person who especially likes soup and who enjoys a bowl of it in all sorts of different situations. And if someone asks us why we like soup so much we'll give them some reasons, and those reasons will be *completely irrelevant.* Yet we will present ourself as—and feel ourself to be—someone who chooses to have this theme of soup in our life because of those reasons. And it will all be an illusion.

Couldn't any neurosis, compulsion, pattern, obsession, psychosis or character disorder be created in someone by implanting the proper combination of post-hypnotic suggestions? Yes. Why is this important? *Because early experiences in life function essentially like post-hypnotic suggestions.*

When we're experiencing the shock and pain, physical or emotional, of a deeply perceived threat to survival then whatever "suggestions" are present at that time will be burned into our mind just as if they were post-hypnotic suggestions. And even though forgotten, they will affect us subsequently in just the same way.

For instance, a husband and wife quarrel violently while a young baby girl watches. The husband leaves in a rage, accidentally knocking against the baby, and the wife mutters at his back, "You bastard!" The baby experiences a threat to survival from the violence of the scene and from the loss of her father for a few days.

Yet the mind of the baby notices that it survived. By the logic of the primitive mind, therefore, survival was *achieved* by a quarrel where daddy left. The "post-hypnotic suggestion" the baby picks up is that people similar to daddy—i.e., tall men with dark hair, let's say—are bastards, and that one survives by entering into a relationship with one and then causing him to leave. And later in life, that is exactly what this baby-turned-woman will do. And in each case she will have brilliant reasons for causing things to turn out that way. And of course the reasons will look like reality; they will look like the truth.

Absurd? Yes. Nonsensical? Yes. Destructive? Yes. But to the mind, effective for survival? Yes. The mind equates that behavior with survival and will create that situation over and over again in order to "survive." Look around and we'll see people (including ourselves) creating recurring patterns again and again in their lives.

These patterns in our lives are absolutely non-nurturing and yet we are all frozen in them, clinging to them—and clinging to all our brilliant reasons as to why our life keeps turning out this way or that way.

Watch the recurring themes and patterns that run our lives: some of us make our lives about trying very hard but never quite making it. Some of us are habitual victims of one thing or another. Some of us become chronic complainers or bored cynics or righteously indignant crusaders.

Some of us make our lives about getting others before they get us. Some of us smile a lot while feeling lonely inside. Some of us make our lives about producing guilt in others through self-sacrifice. Some of us make ourselves the central figure in an ever-recurring tragic drama. Some of us use being "on" as a means of not really being with others.

A list of the different themes and patterns that run our lives in various ways would be virtually infinite. And each one is no different in quality from the post-hypnotic suggestion about having a bowl of soup. Each is mechanical, automatic— and yet accompanied by all sorts of voice-overs, all sorts of reasons and explanations. We get stuck in these patterns, frozen in them, just as if we were to emphasize a few notes on the piano over and over.

The payoff in this automatism is survival, and survival means being right. For example, the baby who heard her mother say "You bastard!" as her father left the house is now, as a woman, engaged on an unconscious level in proving that men are bastards. And when through her unwitting behavior each love affair breaks up abruptly and that man leaves her too, she gets to be right again. She gets to feel self-righteous and self-justified. "See? I told you. Men are bastards."

Since the mind is nothing but this collection of tapes, positions, patterns, programs, points of view—all names for the same thing—getting to be right about them is tantamount to validating the existence of the mind. Since the mind is its points of view, then perpetuating them, running them, being justified about them is the very act of survival itself. It is identical to perpetuating the "I." "You" and "I" survive by running tapes, by getting on positions and being right about them.

Of course, methods exist for improving this situation. Going back into one's past, locating and re-experiencing the incident that burned in a recurring pattern in one's life will cause the pattern to cease running, just as re-experiencing the moment when a post-hypnotic suggestion was implanted will cause that suggestion to cease also. This is Patanjali's *prati prasov* method, and in the West exists as various forms of regression analysis.

Another method is to consciously focus one's attention upon the complex of attitudes, body sensations, postures, expressions, points of view, conclusions and images associated with a recurring theme or pattern in one's life. In its various aspects, this is the method of psychotherapy, and works to give us some insight into our patterns and thus to lessen their force and power.

These methods are valuable in helping us to adjust to life. But while they can ameliorate some of the problems that we humans create for ourselves, they cannot relieve the deepest suffering of the mind because they don't involve a deep seeing into the nature of the mind itself, which creates its suffering by saying that its stories mean something.

Even if these methods could deal with all the patterns set up by intense threat-to-survival incidents—very unlikely since there are so many of them—they would still not lead to no-mind, to liberation. Why? Because liberation is not of you and I; it is from you and I.

 *Chapter Nineteen*

All methods, all devices can be valuable because they have the potential to begin to rouse us from our slumbers, they can create the critical mass where witnessing begins, they can be a door out of the box in which we spend our life. On the other hand, any method, any device can become a trap if we become attached to it, if it becomes one more link on the treadmill of improving, changing, seeking, achieving...all the material around which the ego condenses.

Anything can be the prison, anything can be the first step into the eternal, into liberation, and it depends upon our willingness to watch. We become enlightened not by what we do or don't do, but by watching what we do or don't do. If we cling to a method it cannot help us with the real problem. And what is the real problem? That we're trying to survive and improve something—our separate selves—which at the deepest level are an illusion, which don't actually exist.

Only awareness doesn't feed this doingness of the mind, because only awareness is not an activity and doesn't keep the mind's motion going. Only awareness is silent, effortless, passive, not of the mind. Only awareness cuts at the root by watching the very nature of mind itself.

For example, let's suppose we're running a tape that men are bastards and thereby creating a situation where our current lover will leave us, making us right again. Good; let's not change anything. Let's simply watch this process without encouragement or condemnation or any evaluation at all.

Let's simply watch as we set up the situation. Let's watch as we create ourself being right. Let's watch as we tell ourself that men are bastards. As we watch, these tapes will start losing force, they will start disappearing of their own accord. We don't need to do anything. Indeed, anything we do is simply another tape.

We just become a witness to our positions, patterns, presentations. We notice them as positions now instead of as reality. We see that our version of reality is being generated internally moment-to-moment by the automatic programs of the mind.

"That bastard!" If we're running that tape, for example, what's real for us is that he's a bastard—until we notice that it's just a story, a position, an automatic product of the mind. Actually, he just did whatever he did; that is what is. On top of that we add our interpretations, judgments, programs, etc. and project them out there.

We see wrongness *out there* and want to change it or be mad about it or whatever. But once we see that wrongness—and rightness too—is being manufactured internally by the mind's survival programming, and that it's merely the mind dreaming, then the wrongness and the rightness, the labels and interpretations and acts gradually disappear.

Then we can simply be with what's there—a child, a flower, a tax form, a lover, a sunset. In that moment there are no obstacles between us and Existence in all Its many forms. The very obstacles become channels.

Without awareness we suffer even if all is seemingly okay on the surface. There's nothing wrong in that, but we pay a price. The cost is being frozen in our mechanical series of presentations. The cost is being dead while we're still alive, dragging along, acting out programmed dramas.

Dragging along in life is heart-wrenching. For the cost of dragging along is missing the mystery and loveliness of Existence. Existence is knocking, but we're not at home to answer the door.

Instead we're off with our stories, dreaming with them, hypnotized by them. We can miss our own life in this way. We can miss the wholeness, the fulfillment, the effortlessness, the bliss that is waiting. We can miss experiencing ourself as the Ocean and not the wave. We can stay entangled in a fight for survival, security, pleasure, rightness.

Let's become a witness to the mind in our daily life. Let's become aware. Let's let everything be grist for the mill. Let's observe our thoughts coming and going just as we might observe cars on the street coming and going. And in addition, using whatever posture allows us to forget the body without becoming sleepy, let's take some time out each day to just sit quietly with no activity. In the stillness and silence of sitting quietly, the mind will come to seem more and more flimsy, distant. And one day it will simply be gone.

A question: If awareness is not a doingness of any kind, how do we start? How do we get it to begin? Actually it's there already, so beginning is really a matter of allowing it to be there. It's simply an allowing. It just happens when we're aware that it will.

Many things happen which we don't understand. And there's no need to understand them. Let's watch. How do we eat? By moving our hand with its utensil to our mouth. Yes, but how do we get our hand to move? By contracting the muscles in our arm. Yes, but how do we contract the muscles in our arm? By sending down a nerve impulse from the brain? And how do we do that? Ultimately, we don't know how we accomplish even a simple thing like eating. We just eat. It just happens.

When we look deeply we see that everything in our life is like this. Things happen, but at the deepest level we don't know how.

Awareness is the same. It begins by itself, and we won't understand it. We can just allow it. We just become a witness to our own movement. There are no instructions.

Opening

Chapter Twenty

We're always seeking. That might be the best definition of a human being: the seeker. We're looking for ways to survive, to be secure and powerful, to be gratified and fulfilled. As we have seen, the mind normally never stops seeking. It is its very nature.

In sum, each of us has certain stimulus-response programs which are predominant and which determine what can be called our prevalent theme or pattern or racket in life. It is our predominant attitude.

For some of us the habitual response may be anger. For others the habitual tone might be cynicism. Some of us have a life which is about trying very hard. For some the habitual tone is grief. Some of us stuff down our emotions and become very monotone. Many other examples could be given.

The tone is not always apparent, but is always there as an undercurrent. Our predominant theme or pattern in life is our mode of survival moment-to-moment, our unconscious method of coping. According to our programming, it is how we seek to survive.

Along with this predominant pattern or survival-mode, each of us has a predominant method or complex of methods for seeking happiness. This is how we feel we can achieve fulfillment, completion, satisfaction. It's our dream, our search. It's our path. If the survival-mode is our way of seeking to avoid the stick, then this is our predominant way of seeking the carrot. It's the rainbow on the horizon for us.

It takes many forms. To some of us, happiness means obtaining enough money—and of course, "enough" is almost always a bit more than what is available. For others, the lure is power. For still others, fame or notoriety. Some dream of achieving a life situation where ever-new sensual experiences can be created. Belief in a movement or cause or way of life is the carrot for some, and the hope is for the triumph of that movement or cause.

Or the path can take a more down-to-earth form. The right degree will make us happy. Fulfillment will be achieved when the perfect lover or soulmate is found...or married...or re-married. To some of us, the holy grail is good health. To others, the advancement of the arts. To be able to retire. The list is endless.

Our path here is that which we think of as bringing happiness once it is perfectly achieved. Once it is perfectly achieved, we tell ourselves, all seeking will end. It will be enough. Of course, there are always barriers or obstacles to the achievement, otherwise that which is being sought would already be here. So the mind's thinking runs something like this: "Once I get this, I'll be happy." "As soon as I get over the hump, I'll relax." "Once I get past these obstacles, I'll be able to enjoy myself."

Now the interesting thing is that sometimes we do reach our goal. We achieve what we wanted to achieve. And what happens? We're gratified for a little while. But then we make an interesting discovery. We discover that our achievement is perhaps not enough after all. We find that we still feel a gnawing dissatisfaction.

And we even see the cause of it. It is because we overlooked something, something that we very much need to be happy. Whatever this something is to us—the right job, the right place to live, the right man or woman, whatever—we now set off to achieve it.

And so the search continues. It has to be so, for that is the nature of mind. What we've done is to exchange our old path for a new path. Before, let's say, what was most important was the spread of the movement we were involved in. Now we know that that was not quite correct. Now, let's say, we know that the most important thing is to own our own house. And so we have a new path now, a new rainbow-goal to reach.

Each new path starts out as a fragrance, as a game, as something pleasant to pursue. It ends in misery and suffering, as we become more and more attached to our path. Before, we were like a dog chasing its tail. Now once again, we're chasing our own tail. The only difference is that since the tail is now decorated a little differently we think it's a different game. As our attachment grows and we whirl around faster we descend further into suffering. We don't have what we want, or we're afraid of losing what we have.

97

If our attachments cause suffering, why do we cling to them? Because all our attachments feel comfortable on the surface. We like our attachments. We get a payoff from them. We get a sense of certainty from them, a sense of comfortable familiarity, a sense of being right. We identify with them.

As the master Adyashanti says, we get a thrill from our desires; that's why we follow them. We enjoy the excitement of wanting something; if the excitement of wanting weren't there we might start losing track of who we are. When the freedom of emptiness starts staring us in the face, it can be very scary. We go back to our wantings and attachments and identities as to a safe refuge.

We feel a desire or an attachment as part of us, as a part of our identity, as our point of view. We cling because our path is our hope of happiness, it is what we think will make us feel good. No wonder we can't imagine giving it up. It would be like wrenching out a tooth, only much more so. We feel as if we would be giving up a part of who we are.

And all attachment involves exclusion. It involves the limited, the partial. We cling to something because we're afraid to cling to nothing. The latter would involve insecurity, falling into the abyss, stepping into the Unknown moment-by-moment. We normally shrink back from that. The Totality is scary to our mind because the mind cannot comprehend it. So we cling to the partial, missing the bliss of the Whole.

 *Chapter Twenty-one*

Beneath the comfort and certainty on the surface is tension and anguish, which is the hidden part of the iceberg, buried deep in the unconscious part of the mind because we normally don't want to be aware of it. Yet it's there, and in unguarded moments we allow ourselves to feel it. Our attachments cause us to live in the future, missing the moment. We live in our dreams, missing the enoughness of Reality, missing the suchness of Existence.

The mind is like a thirsty person who dreams of drinking water but doesn't drink it, thinking that the dreams will slake the thirst. Or it's like a person who studies all about water and imagines that knowledge of water is the same as drinking it. The mind is like a hungry person who instead of eating is always reading the menu. It imagines the delights of eating, but doesn't eat. It dwells in its stories.

What is the way out of this dilemma? Every seeking for a new answer, each renewed search for happiness only keeps us stuck in tension and suffering. Do we then forcibly give up our attachments? Do we reject them, run away from them? It doesn't work. To reject something is still to be attached to it; it's just the opposite side of the same coin.

The attachment is still running us; we're still at the effect of it. That is why force doesn't work, because it doesn't really alter anything. It alters the arrangement, but not the inner essence.

For instance, if we force ourselves to give up cigarette smoking we'll still be at the effect of cigarettes. We'll crave them and the attachment will show up in other areas. We may chew gum or eat candy. We might be nervous, irritable. We might yell at our family, or gain weight, or whatever.

When an attachment is renounced we're still attached; otherwise what is the point of the renunciation? Then the attachment will simply move somewhere else. It will take a new form. The energy of the attachment remains, because energy can neither be created nor destroyed. It simply moves. If it does not move upward into greater consciousness then it will move into a new attachment.

The unfoldment of freedom is awareness. All doing-ness, all attempts to do something about our attachments lead only deeper into the mind, because all doingness is of the mind. Only awareness is not a doingness, not a new goal. We simply see that we've gotten caught again, and the nature of what has caught us. No need to reject the attachment, which wouldn't work anyway—a doingness. No, we just see it. Then the un-attachment happens. The tape disappears.

Each new path is like a drug trip. It feels good at first, we get high on it. But after a while it becomes obsessive; we cling just to avoid coming down. "I'll be able to relax as soon as I achieve such-and-such."

Awareness is seeing that this version of reality—the one we're running now—isn't reality either but just another story, another dream. It's seen and accepted for what it really is. And in that moment of clear-sighted seeing the dream loses its force; it is transcended. Suddenly it drops away from us, like a toy from a maturing child. We didn't reject anything. Just in the observation, things can fall away—or stay.

As the current clinging either falls away through awareness or is rejected because of disillusionment, it is replaced by a new path to happiness. The illusory nature of all paths, all searches, all paths, all doingness isn't apparent right away.

So we couldn't find the door out of the room that way, now we look for it this way. We become aware, perhaps, of the illusory nature of *that* path, but now we get sucked into *this* one. So our life can be a series of substitutions, continuing to substitute new dreams for the old ones.

No path is ultimately "bad" or "good"; there is nothing intrinsically wrong or right about any path per se. Setting up goals and paths is what mind does—that's what is. To reject that process would be like rejecting a cloud—foolish.

We see the story/tape for what it is, then we're no longer fascinated by it. We include it, make room for it, choose it to be that way, love it for what it is. Then it becomes flimsy, it becomes less relevant, it stops running our life.

The path is never the problem. It is not the path but our unconsciousness that keeps us trapped. All paths are good not only for whatever value is there, but also in the sense that they provide opportunities to see through them too.

PART THREE

All devices, all therapies can be useful. All are channels to Reality as our awareness becomes more real. Awareness makes our moment-to-moment living—just as it is—the road to heaven.

Chapter Twenty-two

If we're fortunate, we sooner or later begin to see that all materialist paths—that is, all paths that involve trying to manipulate our environment—do not lead to happiness. Then our search takes on a spiritual form. This is very significant, and it opens up a danger too, because attachments to spiritual paths are more difficult to see as attachments.

Now we're searching for enlightenment or heaven or God or no-mind or whatever the name is. As Osho points out, this is the same movement. Again, we become attached to our path, to our method. The attachment now may be to a teacher or leader. It may be to forms and rituals and dogma, or to a particular growth or consciousness movement.

It may be to a particular organization of seekers. It may be to a set of consoling beliefs, or to sacred scriptures. The attachment may be to beautiful or terrible images encountered during meditation, or it might be to psychic powers developed in such meditations. Inevitably there's a certain metaphysical formulation involved, a certain way of looking at things, and we can become attached to that.

The attachment may be to serving others or to saving the world. It may be to a certain way of acting—very loving, or very high, or very surrendered. It may be to the rapture found in certain absorption states. All such attachments are accompanied by an attitude of "I've found it" or "I know the right way."

Thus we may become also attached to proselytizing—not seeing that attachment to converting others covers over a deep doubt within. Otherwise, what is the need? Otherwise, we simply share what we have like a flower sharing fragrance. There's no concern about the outcome, there is no compulsion to convert others.

Spiritual attachments are more difficult to drop than material ones precisely because they're less dense, less solid, more transparent and thus more difficult to see. It can be more difficult to see them as a dream, as just more of the mind's tapes, as just more of the mind's clingings.

Very often our spiritual metaphysics is associated with very reverential thoughts, very sublime conceptions. They feel better than material attachments. We feel now that we've left illusion behind and are on the true road. How, we ask, can these sublime thoughts and feelings possibly be just more tapes and stories? Yet they are. It is still the mind engaged in the old game of surviving by trying to get somewhere, and clinging to something as a means.

When awareness happens in this moment, then seeking drops for a moment, the tapes disappear for a moment. And what is left is nothing, silence. For in that moment of awareness there is no mind, since the mind is just tapes, thoughts. When there are no tapes there is no mind either.

In that moment there's only silence. In this silence we encounter the Existence. It is already there waiting, but we are not silent, we are not absent, so there's no experience of It. Actually, it's not accurate to say that we experience/encounter Existence, since the Existence is always subject, never object, and since in that moment of awareness "you" or "I" are not there. Only the Existence is there. It encounters Itself.

The goal of all meditation, all prayer, all spiritual paths is simply to reach this point of silence where the mind is not. Each method is beautiful in itself in that it quiets the mind, it gives us a taste, but then we become attached to the method and in this way the mind survives.

Also, all methods are a doingness and they presuppose that there is some goal we're trying to reach. Methods can be extremely useful in freeing ourselves from other attachments, but ultimately all methods must themselves be transcended. Unless awareness happens along with the methods, we simply continue the same game of the mind at a more subtle level. Only awareness is not a method, not a trap because it's not an activity of any kind, and does not involve trying to change anything.

For instance, surrendering to a lover or an avatar is very beautiful. To surrender is to love, it means making the other more important than oneself. It suppresses many programs and stories because to the extent that one surrenders one has no goals other than to be surrendered, to be in love. It gives us a taste of Existence, of bliss because the controller becomes mostly and temporarily absent.

But who is it that makes the decision to be surrendered? The mind, for all decisions are of the mind. Behind the act of surrender is the mind, alive and well. And too, we can become attached to the object of our surrender, and this also is of the mind.

The act of surrendering is a drug, a program, another dream—a subtle and beautiful one. Nevertheless its effects are not permanent because they have not involved a deep awareness of the nature of the mind itself. The tapes are suppressed but not extinguished, and will return when one falls out of love, when one is no longer surrendered.

Prayer is beautiful, because it too is a form of surrender. It acknowledges that there is something greater than who we think we are, and thus the act of prayer by its very nature is an act of humility, of surrender.

Yet, what is the mind's ultimate defense of itself? It is to set up something which is other-than-itself. The notion of a God that can be prayed to presupposes that She is separate from us in some way. It also presupposes the existence of that which is praying. In the very humility and surrender of the act of prayer can be a subtle strengthening of the mind. Can we hear ourself praying? If so, God has heard it.

Guided imagery is another method, a kind of mental motion picture, a visual story in the mind. It is very beautiful and powerful as a device for therapy, for goal-achieving, for relaxation. It can be a preliminary act to meditation. Guided "meditation" is often confused with meditation itself, but it's not. It's actually a kind of guided daydreaming.

Both prayer and guided imagery are still mind-motions, one with ideas and the other with images. Prayer is noisy still, it's a mental talking. Guided imagery is the visual form of this, a visual occupation, something it shares with hallucinogenic drugs. Except for Teresa of Avila's "prayer of quiet," both can keep the mind involved in its doingness. This can also be so of affirmations—another kind of mind-occupation.

All things have their uses at the appropriate time. All is exactly as it should be. And it's also so, as the saying goes, that "when we give it all up we get it all back."

Chapter Twenty-three

Meditation, on the other hand, gradually quiets the mind. It is more powerful than prayer or guided imagery or affirmations since it marks a turning point—the first step from talking to listening, from visualizing to watching.

To do this, meditation makes use of a particular quality of the mind, which is that the mind can only focus on one thing at a time. It can and does move very rapidly from one thing to another, but at a given instant it can only be occupied with one thing.

If, then, the mind is held to a single object, other things are excluded. So meditation can be one-pointedness, keeping the mind focused and concentrated on one object. When attention wanders from the object we just gently bring the attention back to it. And we do so without condemning our wandering, for to do so would be to wander again. Meditation does not involve thinking or feeling about the object in any way. We just focus on the object without adding anything.

The object of meditation can be almost anything. It can be a mantra or a mandala, an internal image or sound, or an unanswerable question or paradoxical statement (a koan). It can be a picture of an avatar or a particular movement or pose by the body (tai-chi, sufi dancing, yoga). The object can be pain or the breath or a pair of eyes (tratak); it can be a candle flame, the sky, a rock or a flower. The object itself is not all that important. What makes the difference is holding one's attention to it.

A well-developed meditation prevents our tapes from surfacing and thus quiets down the mind. It can give a taste of Reality by keeping tapes and programs out of consciousness. That taste can be a real eye-opener and can spur our efforts on the spiritual path. And meditation can bring about states of intense rapture, referred to as *absorption levels* or *jhanic states*. It can bring about lovely, exquisite images. It can bring about psychic powers of various kinds.

There are many possibilities for attachment here. We can see white lights, blue lights, hear heavenly sounds and see forms of incomparable beauty. We can meet the Buddha or Christ and have a conversation. That is why Zen people call this "going to the movies." If we become attached to these images and sounds, then we're simply on a sensuous mind-trip once more, for all images and sounds are mind.

Still more addictive are the psychic powers one might develop. If we meditate very intensely for a long time, especially in certain ways, then psychic powers can occur. We can develop the ability to leave our body, to foretell the future, to read minds. It is a rare person who will not become attached to such powers and others once developed. Yet ultimately it's just another power trip on a more subtle level. It's still the mind working and in motion.

Seductive too are experiences of rapture in jhanic states, brought about by prolonged and intense meditations. They are states of vast ecstasy, quite overshadowing what normally passes for pleasure in our life.

The state of each successive jhana is less exciting, more subtle and still than the one below. We reach each higher jhanic state by being willing to let go of the grosser rapture of the one below. We see that rapture itself is a disturbance, and we relinquish the more exciting forms of rapture in order to obtain the deeper and more subtle ones. And each higher one can become then the new attachment. But, we may ask, what is wrong with an attachment to rapture?

Nothing is wrong, yet it's still a clinging to the limited; it's still of the mind. The mind is still pursuing pleasure. We've tasted the saltiness of the ocean but we haven't entered into it. The changes brought about are temporary, and when the meditation ends the changes slowly fade. Thus we can become attached to the meditation, to retaining the rapture resulting from it.

Concentration meditation, as it's sometimes called, is a magnificent dream, the most beautiful of all dreams, but still a dream. It's an exotic drug, the mind drugging itself; but it's still a kind of drug and sooner or later we come down from it. It's no different in essence from other drugs we seek—power, money, fame, sex, knowledge, altered realities, cosmic satoris, saving the world, belonging to a group and so on.

Concentration meditation is still a doingness, it is still the mind trying to get somewhere.

Why do we meditate? In order to obtain peace, rapture, enlightenment or whatever label we give our goal. But it is still a goal-process. And who is doing the meditating, who is keeping the attention concentrated on the object? Observe closely and we see once more the fingerprints of the mind; we see the doingness of the controller.

Concentration meditation's effects are only temporary because they don't involve a deep seeing into the nature of the mind itself. The tapes and programs have been suppressed but they have not disappeared. They are still there, and they will surface again when we come down from this special drug.

This is a difference between concentration meditation and awareness. Awareness does not suppress anything. On the contrary it welcomes everything, accepts it all, sees everything for what it is. And in that effortless seeing, that seeing which is non-doing and which is not of the mind, the tapes simply begin to dissolve. There is no attempt to change or improve anything. Awareness is identical with a deep acceptance. But neither is there a decision to accept either; rather, acceptance is simply there.

Another way of expressing this is to recall the difference between active and passive awareness. Concentration meditation is an active awareness; it is an intense watching of the door of the train in order to see one's lover. It's a doingness; it is pointed in a particular direction. True awareness is totally passive, it is merely watching the leaves go by on the river—choosing none, preferring none, clinging to nothing. It is a silence, a stillness that dissolves all things.

Concentration meditation is not necessary, but can be a valuable device. It is useful in that it can create a situation where awareness can begin to happen. In slowing down the mind it slows down the flow of leaves in the river, so to speak, so that a beginning awareness can more readily perceive the gaps between the leaves. But it's not necessary. The essence of awareness is that we start just where we are, with whatever our present circumstances are.

We do not have to do concentration meditations, we do not have to go to the mountains, we do not have to change our present situation. We simply do whatever we're doing, but now with awareness. We begin where we are. But if we don't yet see the nature of the mind's game then concentration meditation can be useful. It creates a situation where awareness can begin spontaneously, and be more penetrating.

Chapter Twenty-four

The same is true of a master. She is not necessary, for the true master is inside us. But the inside master is, in a sense, still asleep, so the outside master is needed. She simply creates situation after situation until we begin to wake up and become aware, until we begin to see the true nature of our situation. She surrounds us with a fragrance to arouse us out of our slumbers and dreams.

Once we begin to become aware, then she assists us to avoid the various traps and attachments that can arise. And a true master eventually assists us to see into the nature of perhaps the greatest attachment of all—the attachment to the master. Ultimately, even the master must be transcended.

A master is not necessary, but desirable. For while we're asleep we're always dreaming that we're awake. To dream that we're awake is the best way to stay asleep. The mind's best defense is to imagine that it's already gone, that we're already awake or enlightened. Without the disturbing fragrance of a master, our slumbers may continue for quite a while.

An interesting attachment is the feeling that we have to save the world. The world doesn't need saving because it's already perfect.

As Byron Katie says, How do we know that the way the world is is for the highest good? Because it is that way. How do we know the world should be the way it is? Because it is that way. Simple. "Saving the world" can sometimes lead to force, violence, fanaticism. Immense ˌsuffering throughout history has been caused by those of us who were intent on saving the world by converting it to some cause or other.

Let's observe. We see the mind at work, for this is just another form of doingness, of striving. The feeling that the world needs to be saved somehow is a deep non-acceptance of Existence as it is. It is the mind creating imperfection and wrongness *out there* and demanding that it be changed *out there.*

This is the same disease of living in the future. Now the whole world must struggle toward some glorious imagined utopia. What is herenow is never enough to the mind. It can never see that nothing needs to be achieved.

But if nothing needs to be achieved, why then does a master bother to teach others? Because the master has no achievement in mind; they're simply sharing who they are.

A true master is like a flower that has bloomed in the desert. The flower gives off its fragrance not out of some compulsion but because that is its nature, that is what it does. The fragrance will be there whether anyone notices it or not. And there is no choice about it. If someone passes by, the flower does not determine whether it likes the person or not before it shares its fragrance; nor does it ask itself whether it is liked. No, the fragrance is simply there.

And the fragrance is not given off to help you or save you. It is simply there out of the flower's abundance, out of its bliss and exuberance. The master is the same.

What's the master doing? Actually, he is not teaching at all, for there's no doctrine or body of knowledge to convey. That is why a master never really gives an answer, but simply destroys the question. Because he is not out to teach us some knowledge. Instead, he is out to destroy our mind.

The effort of the master is to pull all supports out from underneath us until the mind has no place left to stand. All answers just fill our mind again, so how can a master give us answers? And since he's not giving answers he's inexhaustible, he can go on forever. A body of knowledge is limited, but a master is unlimited. He knows nothing; he has attained to perfect ignorance, so he can keep on talking for all eternity and never exhaust the subject.

 *Chapter Twenty-five*

It's said that a master is awakened, but what does that mean? What does it mean to be a master? What is this thing awakening? Is it some kind of insight? Is it formulating the final system, achieving the ultimate solution? Is it reaching the final goal?

None of those things. Freedom is seeing that there is no goal at all. It's the dropping of all goals, of all seeking. It's the dropping of all attempts to improve, get better or change. But this dropping is not a doingness or decision. Rather, it is a deep seeing that all attempts to get somewhere in any way only lead nowhere, that they only lead further into the mind.

It is seeing that all attempts to solve the problem, to improve, to survive, only perpetuate the problem and deepen it. It is seeing that all such attempts to solve the problem are the problem itself, and that the problem is an illusion, that it doesn't exist except as attempts to solve it. All striving of any kind, therefore, simply falls away.

It is a moment when all doingness simply drops. Not that we drop it. We simply see the true reality of things and in that moment the doingness drops away of itself. This doesn't mean that we necessarily become inactive.

Instead, it means that we do whatever we do—without strivingness, without compulsiveness or concern. We've been chasing our tail in a thousand different ways, whirling around faster and faster. We're dizzy from the chase, insane. Suddenly we see that the tail cannot ever be caught, that in fact the chasing is the problem and that there is no problem outside of the chasing.

In that moment we simply stop. All the doingness stops. We simply sit down, take a rest and let the dizziness clear. In fact the dizziness and insanity were part-and-parcel of the chasing itself. Now they simply drop when the chasing drops. We see that we're flowing down the river and have been flowing down the river forever and will be flowing down the river forever.

Mind wants to be different, unique, special; it wants to get somewhere, to go in its own direction. So it starts trying *not* to flow down the river, it starts trying to go upstream. And then the whole river, the whole Existence seems to be against us. We are trying so hard, struggling so valiantly against the river, but the river just keeps pushing us in the direction of the flow. The river seems so implacable, relentless, indifferent to our plight and our struggle. The river seems to be hostile, actively working against our will and our desires.

Awakening is seeing that we are creating the problem. It's seeing that the river is not against us, it's simply flowing the way it's flowing. And the issue is not whether or not we're going to flow with the river, because we're going to do that in any event. It is vast, and "you" and "I" are atoms.

Rather, the issue really is whether we will struggle or not as we flow down the river. The question is whether we'll become aware of who is creating the struggle in our life. To the extent that we push against the river the river seems to push back, but the river is not the problem.

If there is awareness moment-to-moment of the mind's struggles then moment-to-moment they disappear; then we can listen to our inner voice and cease our struggling with the river. We stop struggling with Existence. Then we're in a deep bliss as we flow down the river. Then we celebrate existence moment-by-moment.

We see that all attempts to improve our struggles are only more struggling. And if we try to stop struggling and try to flow down the river, then we're in tension. How can we try to flow down the river? We're already doing it. It's just a deep let-go, there's no trying or efforting. All trying, all efforting just keeps the game going.

Mind is like a bicycle—it must keep moving or it will fall down. It goes on creating struggle, searching, survival, desire. It creates movement, striving, change, because otherwise it simply disappears, it falls down. Mind is the struggle itself. Without the struggle there's no mind either.

The mind as controller, as chooser, as decider, as the "I" just disappears. It was an illusion all along, it never existed except as the struggle. But the computing mechanism is still there, and it can be used as a tool just as a hammer is picked up and used when needed. The capability to compute is still there, but the computer is silent unless called upon.

If an awakened person crosses a street the computer-brain will figure out the right time to cross. But the mind, the "separate" person is vanished. That which struggled to control, that which thought of itself as the "I" is gone because it was only the struggle itself. Now the Existence, the Self crosses the street. The guests—thoughts, tapes, the mind—took over the house while the host was away, but now the host has returned.

The master does not need to effort. After all, the river flows by itself. Indeed, at the deepest level we are the river. We've already arrived. What are we struggling about?

Chapter Twenty-six

Freedom is a deep seeing that this is it. This is the way it is. This is the way it turned out. Is is is... Things are the way they are. And things are not the way they are not. Right now, nothing can be any different than the way it is. In the next moment it may be different, but right now it can't be any different. And all there ever is is right now. The future never arrives, because it's always just right now.

This is it, this is the way the river is flowing. To accept it is to enjoy it. But the acceptance is not a decision, it's rather a deep awareness that this is the way it is. Love and acceptance are carried within awareness as a seed.

Awakening is seeing that things are never going to be any different than the way they are...until they are. It is seeing that the river is going to flow this way forever...unless it flows some other way. The clouds will go north until they don't. The sun will rise unless it doesn't. All attempts to change or find the answer simply fall away as we become aware of this. At the deepest level, all there ever is to do is to notice the way it is right now, to be fully conscious of it. Then we're in deep harmony with the way things are. We're in deep harmony with Existence.

To use a different terminology, all there ever is to do is to get off our positions. We get on a position, get off it, on another position, off it, on it, off it—forever. It's not as if we get off all our positions once and for all. That would be like trying to eat breakfast once and for all.

No, the tapes will always be running... until they don't. And what there is to do when they come up is to notice them, be aware of them as what they are. Then they flatten, they disappear. We don't do anything with them. We don't ignore them, reject them or try to change them. We simply notice them...like leaves on the river.

The ground from which we perceive things transforms. Before, the ground was unawareness and sometimes we were aware. After, the ground is awareness and sometimes we're unaware. But the circumstances of our life look the same—the same tapes still run, and sometimes we're aware of them and sometimes not...just as before. Everything is the same.

Everything is the same, but it is being perceived in a new way. If life is a bowl of cherries, then the cherries—the circumstances of our life—have not changed, but the bowl itself has changed.

And what is that difference? Before, the bowl—the context in which everything is held—was that certain things needed to be achieved or changed. After, the ground is that this is the way it is, and that all there ever is to do is to be aware of the way it is. Since that is not a doingness, it's doing nothing. But again, doing nothing doesn't necessarily look like inactivity; it looks like just doing what we do.

Just doing what we do, following our inner guidance, without performing our actions as means to an end. Then each action can become a blissful end-in-itself.

It is as if we've been trying all our life to liberate ourself from a room in which we're trapped. And we've been pushing ceaselessly against the door, trying to get out, and it hasn't budged. Our efforts in pushing against the door—the movements of the mind—never flag even for a moment, but it's all to no avail. The door just won't open. Awakening is seeing that the door opens inwards, and that pushing against the door is what has been preventing it from opening.

Or to put it another way, awakening is seeing that the door won't open because it's the wrong door—so why push against it? But it's worse than that. Awakening is seeing that it's impossible to ever find the right door, and then, seeing that there are no doors at all, just solid walls. And then seeing that not only are there no doors, there are no walls either; in fact, there is no room!

It's seeing that we're already out of the room, because no room is there. The room was an illusion created by the mind so that it would have something to do—to try to get out. But how can we get out of a room when we're already out? This is mind, struggling to get to a place where it already is, striving to achieve a result that's already achieved.

Chapter Twenty-seven

It's been said that awakening is finding out that there's no such thing as awakening. The mind sets up awakening or cosmic consciousness or whatever as another goal, the greatest goal. In Osho's great metaphor, mind thinks that freedom is the top rung of a ladder somewhere. Mind is a compulsive ladder-climber; it carries its ladder around with it and when it finds a good spot it sets it down and starts climbing again. Of course, others need to be elbowed out of the way. And there's no end to the rungs—mind can always create more.

But awakening is not at the top of some ladder, some hierarchy. It's getting down off all the ladders forever. More accurately, it's seeing that the ladders are a creation of the mind, that there are no ladders. So there's no need to get to the top of them, and no need to get off them either.

We're already off—as soon as we see that we are. As soon as we see that we're off the ladders, we see that we have always been off them because there are no ladders. In the instant of awakening, we see that we've always been awakened because there's no awakening to achieve. Awakening is seeing that nothing whatever needs to be achieved, including of course awakening itself. It just happens when it does.

We've been dreaming, and in the dream creating walls, obstacles, barriers, as well as power and money, achievements and pleasures. We've gone quite far away in the dream, to a distant city, and finally in the dream we begin to realize that we are very far away indeed from home.

Then it seems as if it will be very arduous to get back. We begin using various devices...workshops, metaphysics, concentrations, gurus...but the journey back seems endless. We're too far away, it seems...how to get back?

But the problem is the dreaming itself. The problem is that we're still in a dream. In fact, who we really are is already herenow, we have only to awaken to it. It only seems as if we are far away—we have only to awaken and we're back home instantly.

All spiritual methods are simply to change the nature of our dream so that we can awaken from it. Until we awaken, methods and devices are necessary to tamper with the dream...make it more pleasant, less pleasant, more peaceful, more anxious, whatever...until we awaken. Then the dreaming is ended and the devices are too. So a master uses different devices with different people. It depends on what they see in the dream, how they sense that someone's dream needs to be disturbed.

The great teachings stress that awakening happens in an instant. For no preparation needs to be made. It's not a journey, therefore nothing needs to be done. There is no question of changing the circumstances of one's life first, or of changing one's programming. Journeys and preparations and changes all take time; they are all of the mind, part of the dream. No, one simply awakens; it is instantaneous. We just see, no preparation is needed. And in that seeing the concept of awakening itself is discarded. It too was simply a device. In fact, the mind cannot be enlightened. The mind is actually an illusion; with what will we enlighten it?

 *Chapter Twenty-eight*

If awakening happens in an instant, why doesn't it happen to us right now, this instant? Because we—the mind—don't want it to. We want to continue to cling to our goals, our attitudes, our beliefs, our patterns and payoffs. We want to stay in movement. We don't want to be awakened this instant because we would have to let go of the idea that we can control, choose, decide, make things different or better. We would have to let go of who we think we are and what we think we are doing. We would have to let go of "you" and "I," and we're not ready. The dream is familiar, and the problems are old friends—we're not ready.

So, paradoxically, time is needed. There is actually no need for it, but we cause it to be needed. Now time is needed for awareness to develop. It's not a preparation, for no changes are necessary. Rather, we'll continue to cling, but awareness will flower in us by and by...and then one day it will happen. Our awareness will have become strong enough so that suddenly we see through all our efforts to remain occupied. We see that awareness is all that is ever needed or possible, and that our efforts to achieve a result are what have been causing the delay.

This is satori, awakening. But it's not the final, ultimate liberation. It is not the case that after satori we will never run a tape again, never desire again, never again project our version of reality onto reality. Those things will still happen, we can expect them. But the ground has shifted. Now when those things happen we watch them, observe them...except when we don't.

And we've seen that ultimately this witnessing is all that can ever be done, and that it's not a doing. So nothing is being done, nothing is being changed, everything is the same. Yet things begin happening around us. As awareness increases, reality changes for us. We begin living in a different world, even though it's the same world. Problems clear up or are no longer experienced as problems, because all problems at bottom are just due to insufficient consciousness.

As we continue to watch the mind, awareness deepens. And as the awareness deepens, more and more tapes lose energy, lose force, lose reality. More and more of them become transparent and then disappear. It's not that we're trying to make them disappear. There's an acceptance of them, we're perfectly willing to have them there. In that very acceptance, though, they start disappearing of their own accord. And as they start disappearing a great silence increasingly descends on us. We become more and more still within.

And then one day the final, the ultimate happens. The tapes are all gone, they are simply there no more. And we're there no more either. All desires, all goals, all clingings, all programs are absent, extinguished. There is no past and no future anymore, there is only the moment. The ego's smoky candle flame has gone out, but now the sun lights up the sky. We are dead, we are gone, but now God is alive. While we were, God was not. Now that we are not, God is. Existence Itself now dances through the form where we used to be. The inner Melody just moves through us.

This is nirvana, the final enlightenment. And "nirvana" is such a beautiful word, for it means "no burning." There's no longer the burning of desire, of striving and clutching. And in the absence of that, in that utter emptiness there's a quiet bliss that's beyond happiness, beyond excitement, beyond the thrill of any kind of experience. The bliss of Existence Itself.

Now It moves, It controls.

As Jesus said: "Thy will be done."

Silence

Chapter Twenty-nine

Clouds float across the sky. They're not trying to go anywhere. They're not trying to accomplish anything. They are not choosing where to go. They are just drifting, letting the Existence carry them along. There is no decision-making, no trying, no struggle. There is a let-go, but not even a let-go, for there is no controller to let go. There's simply peace. There is what is.

All of Existence is like this. There is no purpose to it, no meaning, no goal. As Osho said, meaning and purpose are constructions of the mind which it imposes on Existence. The mind thinks that Existence has to get somewhere, that there has to be some purpose to it all, that someday some far-flung omega-point will be reached and that was the purpose. But then what is the purpose of the omega-point? Purpose is always an infinite regression, it always depends on something else. What is right now is never enough.

The purpose of Existence is just to be here right now, being what It is. It is totally sufficient in Itself at each instant. It has no purpose except Itself. It has no reason except Itself. The rose is not trying to be something else; it is in bliss to be what it is this moment.

Clouds, rivers, trees, life itself—all of Existence is in a deep ecstasy. All except us humans. We humans are in secret misery because our mind can't accept this moment; we must try to be somewhere else. We must try to control. We must make decisions. The mind is always serious—there are things to be done. Even when we let go, even when we laugh it's only on the surface. Deep down the mind is still serious.

Existence, on the other hand, is playing. It is having fun with no goal. Yes, there is death. There is pain. But death is an integral part of life, it's absolutely necessary to life. Life and death are not opposed to each other, they are two faces of the same thing. Death clears out the rigidity, the calcification, the stuckness, the willfulness, the dead unbendingness and thus makes life possible.

Life is flexibility, it's suppleness, it's the ability to adjust to change, to bend with the wind. A tree begins as a flexible sapling and ends as dried-out stiffness. Without death there would be no life, for there could be no change, no room for life. All would come to a standstill. Death/life are inseparable; they're the same phenomenon.

Similarly, pleasure is impossible without pain. They're inseparable; they're also one phenomenon. The mind creates them, separates them, then tries to cling to the one and avoid the other. Mind can't accept the totality; that's why it misses. When we're feeling pleasure, pain is taking a rest. It's gathering energy, it will soon come to the fore. When we're feeling pain, pleasure is taking a rest and gathering energy; soon it will come.

When the pendulum swings to one side it must then swing to the other, but it remains the same pendulum. Beauty is impossible without ugliness. Good is impossible without evil. Happiness and sadness depend on each other. Love and hate include each other. Dualities come into existence at the same time. Mind creates them. Existence is simply what it is. Mind creates polarities and interpretations about it.

Existence in its suchness is perfect as it is. Which is more perfect, ice or water? All is equal, nothing is better than anything else. Nothing is more important than anything else. Nothing is needed for all to be complete. Which is better, a long blade of grass or a short blade? Both are perfect. The Existence is perfect, and goes from perfection to perfection. This looks illogical. If reality is going to be perfect, how can it already be perfect? This makes no sense to the mind, for the mind is a perfectionist—always wanting to achieve perfection. But how can it achieve perfection when Existence is already perfect? It's an absurd task.

But what about disease, poverty, evil? What exists is what exists, only the mind labels certain parts of it as "bad." Good and bad depend upon our point of view. If we see a cat kill a mouse, that is not evil to us; that's just nature. But to the brother of the mouse it is evil. What threatens our survival or the survival of that which we identify with is "bad" to us; what assists our survival we then call "good." To see good and bad requires a position, a point of view, an identity. When there is no identity and no position there is no bad, and no good either. Then all simply is what it is.

There is no way to foresee the ultimate consequences of anything. That which we call bad may lead to good. That which we label good may lead to bad. Certain monastic orders did many good deeds and also administered the Inquisition; was the founding of the orders good or bad? Drug pushing in Harlem led to capital formation for black businesses. Was this good or bad? The mind is a limited instrument and cannot see more than very limited consequences.

Finally, Existence appears to be a multiplicity on the surface, but that is just appearance, that is the projections and discriminations of mind. Beneath the apparent multiplicity created by the mind, we find oneness...the One. Existence is non-dual. Existence is eternal and changeless and yet appears to change, just as the sky has light and darkness and snow and rain, yet remains itself unaffected by any of it. The One is not poor, not rich, neither diseased nor healthy, neither good nor bad—and that is who we really are, that is all there is.

The One has no attributes and yet has all attributes—It has all the forms of the world. This is the divine dance, the divine play. Beneath each form is the One, is Existence itself, and It is bliss. Existence does not suffer. Except for humans, the forms of Existence can feel pain but not suffering. Only we suffer, because only we compare and desire and feel ourselves to be separate. Only we are attached to things being a certain way—and that's the only cause of suffering. It isn't logical, but it can be seen.

Chapter Thirty

To say that Existence is One is the same as saying that Existence is everything, for if it is One it leaves nothing out. If something were left out then Existence would no longer be non-dual, it would no longer be One.

Similarly, to say that Existence is One is the same as saying that It is emptiness, nothingness, for one can only be understood in contrast to two; if Existence is One then there's nothing to contrast it with, and so it is the same as saying it's nothing.

The ocean is one, but to a fish it's the very quality of existence. There is no way to get outside of it, no way to contrast it with anything else, so to a fish the ocean is nothing, it doesn't exist. If a pencil is expanded until it is everything it vanishes, it becomes nothing. Not only is the One everything, the totality—It is also nothing, emptiness, the Void.

This description can also apply to the person who has reached nirvana, final awakening. They are everything, they are nothing, they are one. They're one because they're unified, they're in harmony. There's no longer any distinction between the conscious and unconscious mind, because everything is conscious.

Such a person is no longer a cacophony of successive mind-states—anger replaced by hope replaced by frustration replaced by gratification, etc. Instead, they are in peace and serenity; they are in a deep harmony with All. There are no longer conflicting elements—love competing with hate, greed competing with fear, happiness competing with grief. Now all of it is included, all is transcended. They are whole, complete, serene. They are One.

Such a person is also everything, the Totality, because there are no longer any boundaries. Trees merge into the sky merge into clouds merge into others. Not that they don't use labels and concepts when appropriate, but they just play with them as utensils, devices. They no longer see the labels and concepts as reality. Reality for them is All, is One.

There's no longer any experiential separation between such a person and someone else. When she helps her neighbor there is no thought of "help," when she loves her neighbor there is no thought of "love." The neighbor is her, she is her neighbor. It is simply the left hand washing the right.

She is also nothing, for she is empty. She is empty of desires, attitudes, models, concepts, positions, attachments, goals, judgments, rigidities. She is empty of tapes, empty of programming. She can use such things when appropriate, but otherwise there is silence within; they do not run her. For instance, if she talks about what has happened to her she will use concepts and positions to do so, but she won't take them seriously. They won't be "truth" to her, they won't be "reality." She'll just play with them.

And if she talks again tomorrow she'll probably contradict what she said today, and deliberately so. For the listening mind will try to box up what she says, to position it, to make it into the "truth." So the awakened person will break up tomorrow the concepts she put together today.

For she knows that what she is talking about can't be contained anyway. What she is really doing is using words to point to something beyond words, she is using structures to allude to something beyond structures. She's hinting, she's using metaphor, she's playing with boxes and structures but doesn't take them seriously. She's not attached to them. Her real message is the silence between the words, the emptiness beneath the structures. She uses words to seduce people into silence.

She's empty of goals. Yet if she goes to the supermarket to buy apples it will appear that she's set up a goal to that effect. But that's only the appearance. It is all equal to her. If her car has a flat tire on the way, that is just as good as the apples to her. She has no preference. She was just playing with the apples and the supermarket, it was just a dance.

If now the dance moves this way instead of that way, it is all the same to her. It is beautiful this way too. Whatsoever happens is beautiful to her, she'll celebrate it. For she is silent inside. She can play with goals, models, concepts, attitudes when the moment arises, but she doesn't cling to them—and they don't come unless she asks them. They do not run her because they don't come uninvited. Besides, she's not there, there is nobody to run.

She is not there because who she was has died. Who she thought she was was her beliefs, attitudes, thoughts, goals, emotions, sensations, desires, status—all of her positions, all the limited things that she clung to. She thought she was her programming. Now all that is dead.

It's not that the computing machinery is not there anymore. It is there, but it computes now only when called upon. It doesn't manufacture stories and behaviors of its own accord anymore. And it's not that the tapes are erased. They are there in storage—she can remember them if she wants to—but now they are memories only. There is no identification with them. They have no reality, no force, no energy. They don't come up of their own accord, in response to stimuli. They come up only if called upon. As they used to be, they no longer exist.

Because the tapes don't exist anymore, she doesn't exist anymore either. Because who she used to be was just the tapes and programs, including ones that she existed separately, that she was choosing, that she knew what was true.

Now she is gone and there is no-mind, emptiness. Now the Divine is there, the Existence is there, the Ocean is there. Because she is gone, God is at home. Now there is no more controller, no more chooser. There never was; there were only tapes with the concept of a controller, a decider. When the controller, the chooser disappeared she disappeared too. Now Existence chooses. Now the Mystery is the controller.

Chapter Thirty-one

Who is beating our heart right now? If we are, then let's will it to stop beating. Who is filtering our blood? If we are, then let's will it to stop for a few moments. In truth, Existence caused us to be born, Existence is beating our heart, Existence is breathing us. It is moving the sun and stars, it is moving the electron around the nucleus, it's blowing the wind and raining the rain.

It's doing all of it—all of it absolutely. Why, then, do we persist in believing that we must fend for ourself, that we must look out for #1? Existence is taking care of our heart; will it not take care of us? Our life is no more than a dewdrop on a leaf, slowly falling off—why all this fighting, ambition, struggling, seeking? We are a drop of rain evaporating in the sun. Let's enjoy it! Can we see our real situation?

Let's look within and let a deep trust arise. Let's let ourself be borne on the back of Existence. Let's let the River carry us. In truth, It's carrying us anyway. Why struggle?

But this is not enough for the mind. The mind finds it difficult to trust. The mind asks, "But what if I die? What if I don't get enough to eat? What if I don't get enough money? What if I don't get the right partner?" And so on.

Mind's questions presuppose certain preferences. But the awakened person has no more preferences. If death comes, good; she'll celebrate it. If hunger comes, good; she'll celebrate it. If illness comes, good; she'll celebrate it. If joy comes, good; she'll celebrate it. If the wind blows through the trees, good; she'll celebrate it. Whatsoever it is, she will celebrate it, she will be grateful for it. And in truth, the River is going to flow wherever It flows anyway. Why not celebrate the way It is, whatever It is?

There is a true story of the Sufi master Bayazid and his disciples who came to a town at night. It was cold and raining and they were hungry, but the townspeople would not let them in. So they went to an adjacent hill, and there Bayazid praised God for his many blessings. One of his disciples said, "Now this is too much, you have gone too far. We are hungry, cold, wet tonight—and you're praising God?" Bayazid replied, "I must praise Him, for He fulfills my needs so beautifully. Tonight I need to be hungry. Tonight I need to be cold and in poverty. Tonight I need to be wet and shivering. Otherwise, why should He give them to me? He takes care of my needs so perfectly."

This is the trusting being. There's a let-go, there is no struggle anymore. In his heart there is acceptance and joy and a deep gratitude for All that is. His gratitude and acceptance are so great that he cannot contain them; they overflow in a profound bliss that is independent of circumstances.

Just to see the sky is too great a gift for him, it overflows into bliss. Just to see a tree blow in the wind or hear the crickets cry is the fulfillment of his being. To eat his dinner or to look into the eyes of another is the meaning of his existence. It is totally complete, moment-by-moment. Nothing is lacking. All is perfect. Simply that things be what they are, that is all that he asks.

Actually, it is not even accurate to say that he is trusting or accepting, for that implies a decision about it. Accurately, he doesn't trust, he doesn't accept, for there's nobody there. There is no one to be trusting or accepting. Simply, there is trust, there is acceptance. There is gratitude, celebration, bliss. They're simply there.

Such a person sees that there is nothing to do and that nothing is needed, so he doesn't do anything. To the mind this sounds as if he lays down and goes to sleep, but in fact it just means that he does what he does. The inner Melody moves by Itself. The Voice moves through that hollow flute.

Chapter Thirty-two

Doing nothing does not have a particular form to it; it doesn't look a certain way. It is not a form or doingness, but a state of mind. More accurately, a state of no-mind, a state of absence.

When a bird sings it isn't thinking about how it must sing today and it doesn't have a goal about finishing its song. It has no purpose in mind, it is not trying to accomplish anything. It's simply singing out of its exuberance, there is no goal or meaning about it. It's doing nothing. The awakened person is the same. He "does nothing" because he is not attached to any goal; his mind is silent, absent.

From that silence he spontaneously does each moment whatever will be most harmonious and appropriate. He does not think about it, there's no decision. He simply does what he does; whatever happens, happens. There is no doingness, there is no effort anymore. All effort is gone. All is spontaneous, effortless, harmonious, compassionate. Yet to someone's mind it may not look that way.

He may strike a devotee, as many Zen masters did. To the mind this looks cruel. But it may be the precise action that will awaken that devotee in that moment, in that situation. It may be the greatest compassion. There is no way to judge it, Existence itself is acting. He may found a hospital, or throw a party. He may teach people how to dance, or sit silently. He may comfort a weeping person. Or he may not;he may want that person to fully experience the grief. There is no way to tell what he will do, or what he should do.

The mind takes the concept of awakening and decides what it would look like, what an awakened master would do and say and act like. And it is like a caterpillar trying to decide how a butterfly should act. There is no way for it to know, for it can only think in caterpillar terms.

Awakening has no form, no structure; it doesn't look a particular way. There are people who think that an awakened being should look always loving or always serene or whatever their model is. But a master may be stern or gentle, talkative or silent, playful or penetrating, depending on the moment. He uses forms, they do not use him. He plays with whatever form is most appropriate to the moment.

The awakened being has no doctrines, no moral code, no set of rules. None are needed. Moral codes are attempts to curb the innate violence and greed of the mind. They are necessary restrictions imposed from the outside since the inside spirit is lacking. A master is absolutely moral, but the ethics is flowing from the inside out and no set of rules can contain it. His morality is a function of the moment; it's a spontaneous, harmonious response. He is not thinking in terms of being "moral" or "good." He simply responds in the appropriate way. He is just natural, flexible.

All other so-called moralities are suppressions of the mind's greed and violence, they are a using of force against force. With the mind in control they are sometimes necessary, but they're not natural.

Humans have become the most unnatural animal, in fact the only unnatural animal. We're addicted to force since we want to change things and we feel it is very important that they be changed. We don't see that all problems reside within our own mind, are creations of our mind. We don't see that using force to accomplish our ends is like trying to pry open a flower by force. Nothing is accomplished except destroying the flower.

Existence is doing it all. Existence opens up millions of flowers everyday, no force is needed. No help at all is needed. What can we do? We can just stay out of the way and let the River flow. It will take care of everything. It already is taking care of everything, we just don't see it. When we drop our struggling and our models of how it should be, we find that It's already carrying us and always has been.

We humans have surrounded ourselves with dogmas, rules, regulations. We create our own prison with our mind, and then cling to our bars because they are familiar to us, they are a known item. Mind feels comfortable with the known, threatened by the unknown because mind cannot exist in the unknown. The unknown is infinite, wild, unpredictable; it is the very fabric of Existence itself. So even though we may be in misery in our prison, we cling to our dogmas and our rules and rituals.

They serve the purpose of reducing the unlimited to the limited. They reduce the unknowable to the knowable. They are familiar, a comfortable misery. Then we try to escape this prison by improving things, including improving our rules and dogmas. This is like decorating our cell with jewels, replacing the iron bars with gold ones. We're still in prison.

The person of wisdom, on the other hand, is free. One of the names for awakening is *moksha*, liberation. She's willing to go wherever life leads her. She knows nothing, and knows that she knows nothing. She has no rules, no guidelines, no security. She plunges into the unknown moment-by-moment. She is surrendered to Existence, she trusts it totally. She is grateful just to be alive, just to breathe. If life gives her bitter fruit to eat, she is grateful for it. If life gives her sweet fruit, she's grateful for it. It's all the same, there's no sweet or bitter. She is simply aware; she watches.

This awareness is the key. If her body-mind cries or becomes sad, she's not identified with it. She's a witness to it, she watches this beautiful flower of sadness. She doesn't try to stop it or push it away or distract herself. She watches it just as she would watch the clouds in the sky or the ripples on a lake. The sadness has its own beauty.

There's no difference for her between inner phenomena and outer phenomena, between emotions passing and clouds passing; she watches both. They are the same—simply waves on the surface of Existence. As she watches the sadness, by and by it disappears like a cloud passing to the horizon. It was beautiful but she doesn't cling to it.

Now she witnesses whatever is next. It might sound as if she's indifferent, but she's not—she's just detached. To be indifferent is to have little or no interest in life. Either life has beaten down such a person and they've become filled with hopelessness, or they've become jaded and cynical about life and it appears dull and tedious.

The person of freedom is not indifferent at all. He is very alive to life. He is filled with it moment-to-moment, whatsoever it is; he is spontaneous. But he's detached because he does not cling to any particular part of life. He lets each moment go to make way for whatever is in the next moment. He is open, receptive, flexible...but not indifferent in the least. He watches all, accepts all, but clings to nothing, identifies with nothing.

He is like an empty mirror. Whatsoever stands in front of the mirror is reflected faithfully. The mirror does not ask whether you are beautiful or ugly, male or female, friendly or hostile, healthy or sick, rich or poor, young or old, powerful or helpless. The mirror doesn't try to avoid you, it doesn't ask you to stand in front of it. It has neither aversion nor desire.

It simply reflects you faithfully when you are in front of it. It is filled with you. But it does not identify with you, it does not feel that its survival depends on you. It is not worried about survival at all. When you leave the mirror does not cling, it lets you go. It does not ask you to stay, it does not cling even for a moment.

The person of wisdom is like this. His consciousness is empty, silent. If something comes into his consciousness he accepts it, loves it, is grateful for it, but doesn't cling to it. Even to say that he does these things is inaccurate, for he is not there. Rather, the acceptance, the love, the gratitude is simply there.

Even to say that they are there is inaccurate, for there is no concept that they are there. There is just a perfect reflection of what is there, an unstained consciousness of what is there, a choiceless mirror-like awareness of what is there— and this is the acceptance and love.

Chapter Thirty-three

Love is often thought of as something we do. But have you ever tried to love? It feels shallow, false. Whenever we are trying to be some thing, it means we're not that thing. Otherwise, what's the point of trying? If we're trying to be pregnant, we're not. If we're trying to be loving, we're not loving. The very effort of trying means it is not genuine, it is not natural. Love isn't a trying, it's not an attitude. It is not an activity. It's not a shining glow in the eyes, and it's not a melting feeling. And it's not an intoxication with someone or something.

Love isn't a feeling or a point of view or a doingness. It has no form to it, it doesn't look a particular way. The mind doesn't love, for love is possible only when there aren't any attachments or objectives, when the moment alone is everything. It is the Self that loves.

Love isn't something that has to be achieved, not something that has to be put into place. It is always there. Always it is there, but it's obscured by mind just as clouds obscure the sun. Let the mind fall away through awareness, and suddenly love is there, it is already there. It has always been there. It is the bottom-line. We can't do it. Yet become still inside and it is already present. When mind is absent, love is present.

Since love is at the level of the Self, it has no form to it. It's like a fragrance emanating from a flower. It is there; we may partake or not, as we wish. It's like a gentle rain which waters good crops and bad crops alike. It has no preferences, it makes no choices.

It is unconditional, it asks for nothing in return. On the contrary, it's an overflowing, it has too much already. It is like rain clouds pregnant with water; there's a gratitude that the thirsty earth is willing to receive the rain. It is like an orange blossom heavy with nectar; it is grateful when the bee takes some. Love asks for nothing. What could it ask for? It is already full, it is overflowing.

Love doesn't try to possess, for it doesn't need anything. It allows perfect freedom, for nothing is needed in return. If something is needed—some commitment, some expression of gratitude—then it's not love. Love and freedom are not separable; they're two wings of the same bird. Possessiveness is always of the mind; it is about being unfilled, about lacking something. Love is full, it doesn't cling. It will not try to hold anyone. It accepts whatever is, each moment. It's not attached, it has no preferences. Like the sun, it shines on all things.

To love, the quality of all relationships is the same. The quantity may differ—more time may be spent with some than with others—but the quality is identical. The mind rebels at this, for it always wants to be special and unique and to focus on the special and unique. But to love, each person has the same essence; indeed, everything in Existence has the same essence.

True love is non-directional, therefore. It's not directed towards particular persons or things; it has no address on it. It is open to everyone and everything.

Love is easily misunderstood by the mind. For instance, the mind may decide that it is very loving now and that its love is unconditional. This has nothing to do with love, for real love is unconscious of itself and has nothing to do with decisions or self-image.

Alternatively, mind may interpret having no preferences as some formula about sexual promiscuity or celibacy. This conceives of love as an activity or a denial, and it's neither one. Romance, sex, renunciation are all drugs, intoxicants; they are a doingness and we come down from them. We don't come down from love because it is not an up.

Love is not hot as passion is. Neither is it cold. It is just in the middle—a quiet, subtle, warm fragrance which can't be practiced or implemented, but which expresses spontaneously when the mind is no longer there.

Chapter Thirty-four

Acceptance is also easily misconceived by the mind. "So if all things are perfect then I might as well hurt or deceive others—what difference does it make?" Such an attitude sees acceptance or its lack as a decision. But acceptance just arises on its own when the mind is silent. So it has nothing to do with any conclusion by the mind that hurting or deceiving others is okay. Such a decision would merely be another tape of the mind, more of its survival programming.

This does not mean to stop doing what we do. That would just be a suppression, a violence; the thwarted energy will not go away but will distort us, it will show up in some other form.

If we eat meat, we might continue to do so but now eat meat with awareness. If we deceive others, we might continue to do so but observe ourselves as we do it. Let's watch. Let's observe. If we're a thief let's add awareness to our thievery—it will fall from us, for it's not possible to steal consciously. Let's not try to change ourselves or blame ourselves, because all that is the usual game. Trying to change ourselves hasn't worked and won't work at the deepest level. Yet in becoming aware, certain things fall away from us.

If we force ourselves to give something up then the desire will still be there, just suppressed. But as we become aware, certain things just fall away. There is no effort, no struggle involved. Those things that drop away are "sins." Those that don't are "virtues." It's a natural process.

Ultimately, the attempt to fight or suppress "sin" or the undesirable is an attempt to fight with darkness. But at the deepest level, as Osho points out, darkness does not exist—it's just an absence of light. How then can we defeat it? How can we defeat something that fundamentally is an absence?

The mind says in effect, "I must get rid of this darkness first before I can turn on the light." Can we see what the mind is doing? We don't need to bother about the darkness in our life or in the lives of others, it's a futile struggle.

Far more effective is to turn on a light.

When the light is turned on, darkness vanishes. There is no need to fight with it; no effort is needed. A room can be dark for many years, yet it still takes only a moment to turn on the light and then the darkness is gone.

Fighting sin is like fighting an enemy in a dream. We don't need to defeat him; we can just wake up. If we're being harmed by others, or if we're the one doing the harming, or if we're harming ourself, we can put our focus and energy on turning on a light in the situation.

What is that light? It can be finding a positive goal that all can put their energy toward. It can be a love warm enough to dissolve barriers and hatreds. It can be looking within to see how our own stories are perpetuating our separateness.

In doing this, any type of rigidity that we try to impose on ourself or life is again a suppression, a form of violence. Life is flexibility, openness, a plunge into the unknown each moment. How can this occur if we're frozen into a structure? A slavish devotion to rules or discipline can make us dead inside. Even awareness can be made into a discipline if it is approached rigidly; then it is not awareness because it has the smell of effort, of tension. The whole point is to become less and less tense inside, more and more open and relaxed.

Like anything else, rules and disciplines can be useful as devices. They can alter the dream so that the dreamer may begin to rouse from his slumbers. But whatever we might use as a device, let's relax into it, ease into it, flow with it.

Let's let everything lead us to increased relaxation, for awakening is simply the ultimate relaxation. If we decide to sit quietly from six to seven every morning, for instance, let's approach it as a relaxation; let's let it be a deep easiness. If we approach it as a heavy, serious duty we'll destroy the whole value of it.

If we use discipline on ourself, let's use it with some awareness. Let's watch ourself as we use it; then something will begin to awaken within us. At first it will be very fragile. Thus as awareness first develops, we may want to maintain our discipline just as you would keep a wire fence around a small sapling to protect it. But once the dreamer is fully awake, all rules and disciplines fall away; they're just irrelevant now. An awakened being may look disciplined because of a daily routine or rhythm, but that's just the appearance.

The routine of an awakened person is not a discipline because it's not something imposed. Rather, it's a rhythm that has arisen naturally, spontaneously, by itself. The Melody is moving unimpeded now in that vessel. The light is on.

Chapter Thirty-five

Just be natural, the Taoist master Chuang Tzu says.

"When the shoe fits, the foot is forgotten." He is saying that only when there is struggle or discomfort do we become aware of something. This is the situation of the mind—continually in a struggle, in a discomfort. Let's see the point: How else can it maintain itself? It *is* the struggle, the discomfort. It has no existence other than that. If we're just natural, if we're ordinary, if we're balanced, there is no place for the mind to stand. It must fall.

To be natural means to be balanced, it means to be in the middle. This is Buddha's middle way. Mind always wants to go to extremes, so it can keep moving. First we eat too much, then we starve ourself. Or we work very competitively, and then we go to the other side and relax very competitively. Or first we're a playboy, then we get sick of that and want to become a saint. The mind tends to move to extremes, it often doesn't know where or when to stop. This keeps the mind alive, because by moving to extremes it keeps moving.

The master is a contrast to that. She's balanced, like a tightrope walker. She leans neither to the left nor the right; but stays balanced over the center, not going to extremes.

She has a great sense of appropriateness. She's just easy, ordinary. To be ordinary is a rare quality, for the mind is always trying to be extraordinary. It wants to distinguish itself, it wants to stand out from the crowd. Even humility can serve this purpose—the mind will try to be the *most* humble. This effort to be unique keeps the mind alive, but it is absolutely absurd. The universe is so vast. We're like a grain of sand on the beach trying to stand out from the other grains. Pretty absurd.

The master knows better; she has seen through such nonsense. She's natural, she's easy, she's light. "Easy is right," says Chuang Tzu. Easy in the beginning, easy in the middle, easy in the end. The master is effortless, non-serious, playful. She knows there is nothing to do, so everything she does is "nothing special."

She just does what she's doing—without compulsion, without attachment. It's a good test: Does what we're doing feel aligned deep down, regardless of what's happening on the surface? If not, the message may be that we're fighting the River somehow. The mind can make a tension even out of easiness by making a rule out of it. "Be easy." This won't work. So how do we become easy?

Actually, mind cannot ever really be easy and relaxed because it's always trying to change or control things. Just look: The Existence is vast, infinite, incomprehensible—and we are going to change it? We know better than God how things should go? We make war on Reality—especially in our mind—and then wonder why life seems so difficult.

Since the mind finds it difficult to relax, one device is to use the mind against the mind, to use the mind to go further into doingness. By pushing the pendulum to an extreme—heavy physical exertion, primal therapy, sustained dancing, etc.—the pendulum automatically swings back to the other side and a silence ensues.

In that silence, awareness can arise.

Awareness is the true road to easiness. All devices—concentration, meditations, therapies, austerities, martial arts, whatever—are only to create situations where awareness can begin to arise, where the dreamer can begin to awaken. We can go on cutting a few leaves off the tree in our life, trying to improve this or that, but the leaves just keep growing back. Or we can cut the root.

Jesus said, "I bring a sword." It's all very well to love everything, but sometimes we need a sword too, in this sense: Sometimes when we're sitting for long periods in meditation, "just sitting," we need to face the fear or the anxiety or the boredom and just not move. Just be unmoving in the face of those things that we've always moved away from before.

The sword that actually cuts the root of the mind is this unflinching awareness. What we're doing, the lifestyle we're leading, the methods we're using are of little importance. Awareness of what we're doing is the key. For awareness leads to silence, and silence in turn leads to deeper awareness; at bottom, they are the same. Awakening is going so far into the present moment that you can't get back out.

Chapter Thirty-six

Watch. We'll see that we create our version of reality by what our attention is focused on. "The floor." We just created the floor by bringing our attention and energy to it.

What is the difference between attention and awareness? Simply that attention is directed, focused, while awareness is non-directed, passive. One way of putting it is that awareness is noticing what we notice. It's noticing the labels, discriminations, responses, models, activities, evaluations and demands that constitute our version of reality.

And as awareness develops, it becomes obvious that we are entirely responsible for the reality that we live in, because it's our version of it. God is not responsible. The world is not responsible. We are responsible. Our experience of reality is our own creation.

The world is a perfect echo of us. It is like standing in a canyon. If we shout "God!" we'll hear "God!" back. If we shout "Hate!" we'll hear "Hate!" back. We hear our own projections. The River mirrors our own struggles. For instance, the qualities that annoy us about others are projections of qualities that we ourselves have. Otherwise, we would notice them but they wouldn't have any charge for us.

If arrogance in someone bothers us it's because we're arrogant. If resentment in someone bothers us it's because we have resentment. Otherwise it would make no impression on us, it would be irrelevant, it would have no more significance than the ceiling. The canyon echos us. And this is true in the widest sense. If the world seems violent, let's look within at ourself. What is violent in us?

All this being so, if we truly want to help the world then we can work on ourself. That is where it starts and ends. If we want to improve someone else then we can work on ourself. We'll be surprised—as our own consciousness is raised we'll find that the other person has "improved." They are much more okay now. A miracle!

As our consciousness deepens we gradually find that we are living in a different reality. The game is to work on ourself—not on others, not on the world. The mind always finds wrongness and problems *out there* and then wants to solve them there, but the mind has created the wrongness and the problems in the first place. How can we ever solve something externally which is being created internally?

A special trap is taking any of the concepts discussed here and using them to make others wrong. For example, if we point out to someone that they are running a tape, we are the one who is running a tape—about them. We are the one who is missing. In our universe, *we* are the person who has the opportunity to get off it. And there is no way to get off it and still be right. Working on other people is a good way to stay stuck in the mind. Let's work on ourselves.

Does this mean that we never communicate how we feel if we're upset about something? Does it mean that we don't ever correct "wrongness" if we feel that something can be constructively done? No. The mind is always looking for rules with which to achieve certainty, but no rule is always appropriate.

Let's be a witness to ourselves. What stories or tapes are we running now? How are we creating our experience of the situation? As Ken Keyes said, first become centered and then act. When we're uncentered and upset in any way we'll tend to create turbulence and disharmony whatever we do or say. So let's let our primary emphasis always be our own consciousness. Let's slowly fall silent inside.

When we're silent inside we'll naturally, spontaneously do whatever is most appropriate, whatever might create the greatest overall harmony. There won't be a decision involved, no rule to follow. It will happen of itself. We will literally be living in a different reality, and the world will look entirely different to us, even though it's entirely the same. What used to be problems will no longer be problems.

So let's not try to solve problems while staying attached to our stories. Our individual problems are not the problem. The world's problems are not the problem. A lack of consciousness is the only real "problem" in this world.

Always, our first priority can be to be more conscious of our stories about how others and this world and ourselves ought to be different—and how those stories are creating our sense of isolation and suffering.

When we become more silent within it will all begin to work. We'll experience the perfection of Existence, not as a concept but as an experiential reality. Nothing will be seen as a problem, not even death. For when we're really silent we're gone, we are no more; we have joined Existence Itself. The drop has merged in the ocean.

How then can death trouble us? Death is a problem to the mind, to "you" and "I." How can disease or pain or loss or poverty or suffering or anything at all trouble us when we no longer exist? Only the Ocean exists, and It's not troubled. All we ever were was the disturbance, the mind's movement. When that is gone, we too are gone. And so is death.

When we're silent within we'll be spontaneously loving and compassionate; we will be love, we will be compassion, but there will be no thought of "love" or "compassion." It will just happen. And when we communicate with someone we won't be dumping our tapes and justifications and blame on them, but simply sharing our experience.

Sharing is being responsible for our experience—"I had a thought just now that you're conceited and I turned it around and saw how *I'm* conceited when I'm thinking that about you." Dumping is when we put the responsibility for our experience out there—"You know, you're conceited!"

Dumping activates the automatic mechanisms of others and creates conflict and estrangement. Sharing creates a communion; it makes us real to others, it makes us available. Then we're not trying to protect anything, for example our story, for we've seen that there's nothing to protect.

The mind always feels that certain things need to be protected for the sake of our survival. But what is really being protected? Yes, the mind itself, the survival programming itself. To the extent that we're willing to share ourself with others, to that extent we weaken the hold of the mind and open up space with others instead of shutting it down. And we'll see more and more that what we are protecting isn't worth protecting, and conversely, that what is really worth protecting—the vast pregnant spaciousness and emptiness within that we really are—needs no protection at all.

Chapter Thirty-seven

The person of final awakening is like the open sky. She is boundless, infinite. The bodily form is merely a contact point with Existence itself. And like the sky, her true dwelling place has no walls, no roof and no floor either. How to protect a dwelling place that has no structure and no location?

The liberated person has a body-mind package but she is not that package; she is the void, the emptiness out of which that package has arisen. How to protect an absence, a void? Since it cannot be harmed, there is no need to protect it and no possibility of protecting it. Consequently, the person of awakening is totally open to life, totally transparent, totally receptive to all things.

She says "yes" to all aspects of life without reservation. The mind gathers energy and strength by saying "no" to parts of Existence. This is liked and that is disliked. But the person of wisdom says "yes" to all of it. And nothing is excluded, not even the mind.

For she knows that Existence is a vast mystery which cannot be penetrated. She knows that she knows nothing at all, and so she simply opens her heart. She trusts. She allows the River to carry her, she knows not where, she knows not why. But with that trusting heart she experiences the bliss of allowing herself to be a part of the flow. Just to exist in each moment is a benediction.

He has no attachment to particular concepts or beliefs, and so he's willing to let others have them. He's willing to let others be "right." After all, each concept is part of Existence too, it is perfect in its own way. And each person is a part of Existence, a part of God—so the divine is speaking through everyone.

He sometimes uses the master Mahavir's logic when it's appropriate. If someone makes a statement of some kind his attitude toward it might be, "Perhaps you are right." He lets the other person know that he understood what was said, but he's lost the compulsion to agree or disagree—least of all with philosophical or metaphysical systems. He's receptive to all things large and small, including all concepts, but he's not attached to any. He plays with them as what they are—toys in the sandbox.

He has abandoned trying to know the how or why of Existence or of his situation. he's abandoned gathering facts and data and answers and solutions. He's willing to play with data and questions and so on, but doesn't take them seriously because he has accepted his complete ignorance.

Ultimately, Existence is unknown and unknowable. It is wild, mysterious, infinite, un-boxable. The mind keeps trying to box it up and pin it down, but it isn't boxable or pinnable. We can pin the butterfly down, but then it's not a butterfly anymore; it's dead.

Only the trusting heart really sees. As the fox said to the little prince, "It is only with the heart that one sees rightly; what is essential is invisible to the eye." Facts, data, boxes do not touch what is essential.

Buddha used to tell a story about a man wounded by a poisoned arrow. His friends and relatives procure a physician to pull out the arrow, but the man says he won't have the arrow pulled out until he knows the name of the man who wounded him and the name of his clan. And he won't have the arrow pulled out until he knows the height of the attacker and his village and his race. And he will not have the arrow pulled out until he knows the type of feathers used in the arrow and the type of wood and the type of metal in the tip and many other things. Buddha points out that the man will die in the middle of finding all this out.

This is our situation. We will die in the middle of collecting our data and answers and goals unless we awaken to our situation. We might think we can go toward happiness like an arrow going towards the target. We might imagine it is a matter of getting certain things in place.

But aiming directly toward the target can sometimes guarantee that we'll miss it. For instance, someone lies back in a lake feeling the sun on her face. She's not trying to accomplish anything; she's relaxed, surrendered. And a moment may come when bliss descends on her. We hear about it, let's say, and we go to the lake to find this happiness. We lie back in the lake waiting for the moment of bliss, but it doesn't come. Why not?

Perhaps because we were direct. We sought directly. But Existence is indirect. It moves through hints and whispers, It reveals itself through silence. Only when all seeking is gone and we're willing to wait for all eternity with no striving, no desire, no goal, not waiting for anything in particular but just waiting for no reason—then, in that empty silence, Existence reveals Itself.

The mind thinks it can find happiness, thinks it can find God, thinks it can find enlightenment. But what map will we use? And how can there be a map when there's no address, no location?

When there is no more seeking after anything at all, when there is simply waiting with no goal in mind, then God finds you. The seeker is the sought. You are the goal.

Chapter Thirty-eight

God finds us when we're not away from home. But God can come only to us when we're totally naked. As long as we are clinging to something in our version of reality, God can't come to us. The Unlimited, so to speak, makes contact with us when we're not clinging to something limited.

Sufis tell a story of blind men feeling an elephant. One feels the trunk and declares that an elephant is curving and long. One feels the ear and announces that an elephant is wide and flat. One feels the tail and concludes that an elephant is like a rope. As long as we cling to our partial version of things we can never see the Real.

Another example: Three people walk down the street. One is hungry and notices the different restaurants. One is lustful and notices the appropriate sex objects. One just had a wallet stolen and notices only the thief up ahead. All are on the same street, but all are in different versions of reality.

To see the Real is to be unencumbered by thoughts or desires about part of it; it is to have no identification left with anything partial. And this means to have no attachment even to any concept of God or Existence or enlightenment, because all concepts whatsoever are partial.

How can we leave our partial versions of reality behind when we're so mired in them? Awareness does it. We see that they are partial. We see moment-to-moment that our version of things is only a version and that it is not reality itself.

We observe ourself moment-to-moment—what we are doing, what we are thinking and feeling, how we're reacting towards this and that. As this continues, the thoughts of the mind gradually die down, and we begin to notice the gaps between our thoughts like the clouds parting and allowing a glimpse of the sun. Then we begin to enter the Silence where we encounter Existence itself. And one day when the Silence is complete we disappear and then, in this metaphor, God can truly play the divine Song through us.

The ultimate value of awareness, therefore, is that it leads to Silence and Stillness within us. And in that Stillness, Existence is. God arises. The Self is "born." Existence, Self—whatever the name—was always there but wasn't noticed because of the incessant activity, the incessant static of the mind's beliefs and clutchings.

Silence then, as Ramana Maharshi once said, is the true instruction. There's no teacher like Silence. It is incomparable. Mind is like the surface of a lake when one is trying to see into the depths. When the surface is choppy and agitated, the depths cannot be seen. Once the surface is still and silent, though, the depths can be seen easily. They were always there but could not be observed.

The value of concentration meditations—focusing on an object such as a mantra, an image, a koan, the breath, and so on—is that they can still the waves of the mind and thus give a taste of Silence. However, the effect is only temporary. The mind is being suppressed, that's all; it does not fall, it is not extinguished. Concentrations are an activity of the mind, they are the mind suppressing and drugging itself. They're a form of getting high, and so we have to gradually come down when the concentration ends.

Concentration is an active awareness and not the true, passive awareness. Instead of being an effortless witness to the flow of leaves down the river, concentration is focusing on a particular leaf. It is attached rather than detached, of the mind rather than the Self. Concentration is thinking, it is the mind addressed in some particular direction. Yet it can be a useful device. It can give a glimpse through the door. And its power of focus can assist our awareness in going deeper.

But true meditation is awareness—passive, choiceless awareness, the witness. It is this which can still the waves forever, which can uncover Silence permanently. It is through awareness that a moment can happen from which there is no slipping back, no coming down.

For only through awareness can one see the illusory nature of the mind and its survival-oriented thinking. Only through awareness can we awaken and see that the mind is not actually there, that the tapes are simply what they are and not reality, that the mind as self-determiner does not exist, that the "I" does not exist, that all the grasping and seeking and judgments and aversion concerning the problems of life are the problem itself.

Only through awareness can we see that at the deepest level there is nowhere to go, that the goingness itself was the problem, that this moment is all there ever is and that being aware is what there is to "do" with it.

Beyond this awakening, however, is a final awakening where we simply disappear. This is the final extinguishment of all qualities that we've thought of as ourself. It is total Silence and Stillness, the final annihilation of all thoughts, tapes, programs, desires, disturbances. We can use thoughts, of course, but it is like picking up a ruler to draw a line. When there is no more use for the ruler, it is laid down; there is simply Silence, Spaciousness.

Then we have attained to being a nobody, a nothing. Now rivers flow in us, stars are born in us, the wind blows through the trees in us. There is the bliss of Existence Itself, a bliss which transcends what is normally thought of as joy and happiness in human life.

In this state of final awakening, everything that would have to be given up at physical death has already been given up before physical death. The body is still alive, but now there is no inhabitant anymore. This awakening, therefore, is truly a dying. It is death. Not bodily death, but the death of "you" or "I," the death of the mind, the illusory controller.

It's the death of everything we've ever associated with "you" or "I." Everything has been thrown, nothing is carried any longer. The luggage full of stories and tapes and desires has been put down forever. We leave behind all our burdens, including the ultimate burden—the separate "I."

Now death has no hold anymore. Death is dead, for we have already died. In that death we are reborn, but it is not us. Now we are not, but God is. God has been "born" through our absence. The Existence lives and breathes through the vessel now. It's like the open sky—eternal, deathless.

The Existence expresses through a human form. Then we are Everything and Nothing. We are Oneness and the Void. Who we are now was never born, so it cannot die. Both life and death have been transcended. Such a person, as Jesus said, is in the world but not of it anymore.

And the Ocean itself rises in the wave.

Chapter Thirty-nine

Is an innocent young infant in this state? Is an animal enlightened? In one sense they are because there is no mind, there is no rational-controller. There is no problem about life because there is no past or future, no expectations or models, no concepts or comparisons. There is just life from moment to moment. On the other hand there is strong instinctual, lower-brain programming to survive and avoid extinction. In contrast, an awakened being has no desire to seek or avoid extinction, because the separate "I" has already become extinct.

But this isn't the crux of the matter. What about a cloud or a blade of grass? Now there is no desire even to survive. There is simply the bliss of perfect harmony with Existence. Are they enlightened?

No...and now we come to the heart of it.

There is no possibility of a cloud or a leaf or a wave awakening because they aren't conscious. Only humans—or any other sentient beings—can become self-realized, for only sentient beings are conscious. Only humans or other sentient beings have the capability to experience the hell of consciousness, the hell of mind—and that is what we do experience. But this hell also contains the seeds of another possibility.

To be conscious means to be split, to be divided. The mind is always trying to be somewhere other than where it is. The conscious mind is pulling in one direction and the unconscious conditioning is pulling in another. Or the desire system wants something other than the Reality herenow. One is not whole. This is the anguish, the tension of mind.

As Osho says, entities who don't have sentience have no tension because they're unconscious; then there is no problem. And the free being has no tension because they are conscious completely; then there is no problem either. Only we humans and other sentient beings are partial; only we live in the hell of being divided. But this partial consciousness means also the possibility is there of becoming completely conscious.

Awakening means first going to hell and then coming back to paradise. Liberation means first battling and struggling with the River and then seeing the illusion and ceasing the struggle...through awareness, through silence, through the extinguishing of who we think we are.

The tragedy of the human is that only he or she truly suffers. No animal, no plant, no river can suffer as humans do because there is no mind to struggle, no mind to live in the past and future, no mind to compare and judge and crave. Self-realization has depth to it because it has first known the misery of mind.

This is why a fetus, even though existing in bliss, isn't awakened—it is not yet conscious. One must pass through the pain of partial consciousness before the doors of heaven can open in complete consciousness.

And then deliverance is here, in this life. In one sense, the pathless path to awakening can be considered a regression back through the history of the organism to life in the womb. As awareness deepens, we go back through a psychodynamic stage, bringing consciousness to and disappearing the tapes formed by painful and traumatic incidents in childhood. Then as awareness increases further we undergo a kind of birthing stage, confronting the human condition of pain and suffering, dying and death and the desire for survival—corresponding to the agony of the fetus as it dies as a fetus in order to be born.

Finally, as awareness becomes complete, one goes back to a transpersonal reality. The fetus is in undisturbed peace, undisturbed bliss. It has no sense of "I," no desires, no urge to get somewhere, to control. It simply is, and there is no problem whatever. The awakened person is like this, but there is a crucial difference—whereas the fetus is unconscious, the self-realized person is totally conscious. Both are in bliss, both have no identity, no mind, but one is conscious and the other is not. To have no mind, no ego, no disturbance within, yet to be fully conscious—this is liberation.

How do we reach it? "You" and "I" can never reach it because we are the obstacle. Only when we disappear can it be reached. Indeed, the moment we are not, It is already there. But we cannot attain to our own non-existence; there is no way for us to reach that, for the very attempt to reach keeps "us" in existence. All that can be done is to cultivate the ground—and then it happens of its own accord.

SILENCE

Existence does it. It's like the farmer growing his crop. He tills the soil, plants the seeds and then waits. He must have great patience. By and by, Existence Itself brings the crop up out of the soil. Yet the farmer also makes a contribution. And when awakening happens it's clearly a grace bestowed by the Whole; there is clearly no doer except the Totality. And yet we contribute too, by tilling the ground.

And how is the ground tilled? How is the seed planted? Through the non-doingness of awareness, mindfulness. But awareness can only become fully mature in perfect silence and stillness. So like the farmer, we set aside periods of just sitting silently and waiting. Unlike the farmer, though, we wait not for anything in particular, but for nothing at all.

We are just waiting. Waiting with an open heart, with a trusting heart. We can reach a point where even the goal or concept of awakening is no longer there, where we're prepared to just wait with no end or goal for all eternity. We can reach the point where time drops away from us, when we see our own uselessness, when we see that the world is doing just fine without us and that we've been discarded, thrown on the junk pile. Only when time drops from us completely has the mind also dropped.

We cultivate then the greatest art, the art of just sitting silently. But sitting silently in great awakeness, consciousness, awareness. It's simply stopping, it is simply coming to a halt. It's allowing the waves of the mind to subside, it's allowing the bicycle to come to a stop and then just topple over. It is the ultimate in doing nothing.

And in that absence Existence reveals Itself.
The Zen master Zenrin said:

Sitting silently, doing nothing,
Spring comes and the grass grows by itself.

Sitting silently, doing nothing, we imperceptibly merge into a harmony with the Existence...which is not trying to get anywhere, which is not trying to accomplish anything, which is simply the bliss of being what It is.

Chapter Forty

Sitting silently, doing nothing, waiting for nothing, just waiting—with no end in view, with no goals or desires or attachments, simply being silent and aware...this is how the final awakening comes.

In our ordinary life the mind pulls away from boredom because it needs excitement to stay alive. It knows only two possibilities, movement or sleeping. If nothing is going on the mind is just bored, it wants to go to sleep. But sitting silently, doing nothing is a third possibility—consciousness without occupation.

It is the ultimate facing of boredom. It is going deeper and deeper into the boredom, into the emptiness, into the hollowness beneath all the onion-layers of the mind. It is penetrating deeper into tedium, into silence, into nothing, into lack of stimulation.

It can be done with eyes closed or open-and-unmoving, it makes no difference. The body is put into a relaxed position where it can be still for awhile. And then the essential thing is that we are no longer moving in a particular direction or dimension but are open to all dimensions, all directions...open to whatever is happening, open to the Totality.

An interesting metaphor:

Wakefulness is consciousness plus mental activity. Deep sleep is neither, it is unconsciousness plus mental inactivity. Dreams are activity without consciousness. But silent, open, aware sitting is the most interesting of all—it's consciousness without activity. Appropriately enough, silent sitting is the opposite of dreaming.

In one sense, this final awakening could be described as being in a state of deep sleep while being fully conscious. In the normal waking state of the brain, beta waves of 14-26 cycles per second predominate. In the deep relaxation brought about by various concentration meditations we pass down to alpha waves of 8-13 cycles per second.

Then it was discovered that Zen monks who are experienced in mindfulness meditation pass down while remaining conscious to theta waves of 4-7 cycles per second, which are normally present only during the medium stages of sleep. And awakening might then be characterized as remaining fully conscious while passing down to delta waves of 0-4 cycles per second, which are normally present only during the deepest stage of sleep.

Deep sleep is very beautiful. In deep sleep there are no thoughts, no desires, no tapes, no stories. There is no struggle, no striving. In deep sleep we are not a particular identity; in fact, we are not anything at all, our identity is gone. There is no clinging, no mind, no "I." On the other hand, there is no consciousness either. Freedom is adding consciousness to this state of inner stillness, and living in the world with it.

It is awareness without attachment, consciousness without an object. The only difference between ourselves and a Buddha, then, is that we have something that the Buddha doesn't have. The Buddha merely has consciousness. We have consciousness plus stories and dreams. Final liberation is the complete disappearance of all stories of the mind.

In this state every moment of life is a benediction, a natural gratitude for the overwhelming loveliness and majesty of life. Every moment is a spontaneous prayer, a spontaneous surrender to Existence itself. But there is no decision to do or be these things, for there's no one to make the decision. There is simply emptiness, open sky, and in that emptiness those qualities are just there.

There is bliss because all is as it should be: It's perfect, It's exactly the way It is. In a cloud, a leaf, an animal, a person is seen the Eternal, the Deathless, the Nameless. The face of the unfathomable Mystery is present everywhere.

The whole universe is seen in a river or a blade of grass, and yet, there's no one to see it. It is the Existence Itself now who sees. The old inhabitant and all her sufferings is gone; now God is the only inhabitant. God looks out at God. God sings a song to God. Infinity can be held in the palm of the hand. Less has become more, for there is a grace over the most mundane details of daily life, or over nothing at all.

There is a kind of great drunkenness with life—but no drunkard, for no one is there. There is nobody, nothing. There is simply bliss, peace, grace, enchantment for no reason, no cause. It's just the quality of the Mystery.

In this state life is like the notes of a symphony, in Alan Watts' great metaphor. There is no attempt to get to the end of anything, for each moment is the whole point. Each note is precious, perfect, needed, complete in itself.

The purpose of all of Reality is now gathered into each timeless instant, the eternal present.

Life is now like listening to the rain—each drop of rain a brilliant jewel, the scripture of Existence. There is only the rain, the sound of the rain, the suchness of the rain. There is no mind, no awakening, no awareness, no listener. There is no anything anymore. All things have merged into emptiness, the void...Nothing. Now there is only the pat-pat-pat of the rain itself, vanishing into silence.

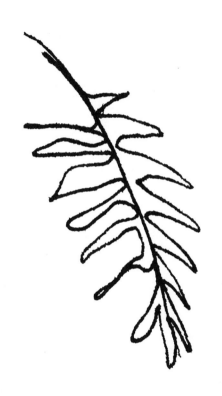

Afterword

The true revolution is always the same. It lies not in attempting to change things to the way our mind wants them to be, but in waking up to find ourselves in love with the way they are. There's no logic to it; it's an illogical falling in love with all of Reality as It is. It's waking up from the dream-sleep of stories and attachments we normally call being awake.

To do this great attentiveness is needed. This brings the transformation. Actually, such mindful awareness is itself the transformation, for nothing additional needs to be done. In that pure fire, certain things will drop away. All things will become new even as we change nothing.

But this mindfulness is subtle. The difference between running the tapes of the mind and watching them as they run is microscopic, a hair's breadth. Yet that difference ultimately is very vast. In other words, it takes a lot of alertness to be alert. And if you're like me, you'll forget over and over.

It's good to allow ourselves some time each day to sit silently, to be aware in silence. In effect, we just sit on the bank and watch the mud in the pond begin to settle by itself—for that is its natural tendency when it isn't being continuously stirred up by the mind's motion.

We don't need to be unduly concerned about the "right" posture, schedule or technique. An undue concern would just create more tension. There are many useful devices, such as verbalizing our watching or mentally sweeping the body, but ultimately they have to be allowed to drop or they become part of the obstacle. Ultimately, awareness has to stand completely on its own. Since it is your unique journey, the natural rhythms that are right for you will eventually find you.

As the mind quiets down—or perhaps more accurately, as it becomes more absent—the infinite Mystery, the undying Intelligence will manifest more and more within us. We can't ever leave It, for It is us, yet paradoxically we journey far afield before awareness or total exhaustion allows us to discover that we have always been home.

I am also on this journeyless journey with you. For all of us, there is no limit to how far we can walk into this limitless, mysterious Ocean that is ourselves.

On this journey to yourself, this pathless path that leads to where you are—to where "you" aren't—may you experience much love. And may you experience the peace that passes all understanding.

Love,

Jimmy

James M. Sloman is an investigative writer whose subject is the human condition. He has sought understanding from a wide range of great teachers past and present, famous and obscure, and traditions ranging from India to the kitchen table.

Originally trained in philosophy at Princeton and with an MFA in film from Columbia, he draws from experience in an eclectic career which has included being a copywriter, assistant editor and computer programmer in New York, a novelist in rural Massachusetts, a trader in Chicago and a market theorist in San Diego.

In addition to presenting occasional courses on theories of financial markets, Sloman has spent over two decades teaching seminars and workshops on spirituality, consciousness in everyday life, diet and nutrition, finding our true calling in life, and accessing our inner guidance. He currently lives near San Francisco.

(This photo was used in the 1st edition
and in honor of that is used here.)

Thank you for reading *Nothing*.
If you liked it, please tell
your friends about it.

Products by James Sloman,
available from OceanBlue
Publishing, include:

May You Be Happy
Handbook for Humans
Nothing
The Ripple
Affecting Our Reality
Songs From The Bottom Of The Sea

Descriptions are on the next pages.

To place an order:

1-800-838-7360

Abroad: (707) 838-6200

Or mail the order form
in back to:

OceanBlue Publishing
98 Main Street
Tiburon, CA 94920

www.ocean-blue.com

MAY YOU BE HAPPY
Blossoming Our Inner Guide
2nd edition, 160 pages, $12

We all want to be happy. And we are sometimes. But then other times we are not. And when we're not, we wonder, why aren't we happy all the time? Why does there have to be suffering?

In *May You Be Happy*, James Sloman uncovers what many of the great teachers of modern and ancient times have discovered, and then clearly, heartfully, and elegantly shares with us their secret of true happiness.

This newly expanded version of *May You Be Happy* is divided into three parts: *Heart, Spirit, Mind.*

Part 1, *Heart*, is grounded in the teachings of Jesus, though a number of other teachers are included. It is about opening the heart and beginning to fall in love with the world.

Part 2, *Spirit*, is grounded in the teachings of the Buddha, though again other teachers are included. This part, reflecting the practical, how-to-do-it emphasis of the Buddha, talks about the inner journey in a number of practical ways.

Part 3, *Mind*, discusses following our inner guide,

our inner voice or knowing, and how to distinguish it from the other voices in our mind. (And other topics including trusting and abundance.)

The emphasis of all three parts of the book is about the gradual blossoming and uncovering of the warm, bright, loving intelligence within each of us.

True unsolicited comments from readers:

"A great job with an incredibly important lesson in the secret of happiness."
—MG, executive

"I have read and re-read *May You Be Happy* and feel expanded and open-hearted with each reading. I will gladly share this with others as it has greatly enhanced my life. Thank you for this precious gift."
—AW

"This is so clarifying, so clearing, it's just incredible. It's just beautiful...Thank you."
—LR, teacher

"I really love it. I'm very happy...It's so beautiful. Incredible reminders for being love, being peace. Great, great job."
—RB, marketer

HANDBOOK FOR HUMANS
A Comprehensive Synthesis of Paths to Personal Growth
560 pages, $24

We get handbooks when we buy appliances and cars—why not one on basic information for living?

"A wonderful new book by Jimmy Sloman is the manual he wishes he had received when he was growing up. *Handbook for Humans* is the culmination of a lifetime of learning and eight years of writing. In it, the author distills the wisdom of dozens of traditional paths to health, happiness, success and peace into an easy-to-digest overview of how our lives really work. *Handbook for Humans* succeeds as an excellent guide to help us achieve balance, equanimity, vibrancy and wholeness in our lives. We recommend it highly."
—Patti Breitman, *EarthSave Marin*

Handbook for Humans is actually a collection of four books in one cover, addressing the *Spirit, Mind, Heart* and *Body*. Each of these dimensions is then divided into an inner and outer area, allowing the reader to clearly grasp the inner work that will support the expressions he or she would like to take into the world.

"If there were only one book you could read to navigate your way on the path of life, *Handbook for Humans* would be the perfect choice. Jimmy Sloman has created a treasure trove of wisdom...that feeds the soul and body. I am grateful for this book."

—Susan Smith Jones, author of
Choose to Live Each Day Fully

Peppered with dozens of real-life stories along with fables, folk tales, quotes & studies, *Handbook for Humans* is the manual many have been looking for to use in daily life as a course in what works.

"...I complimented James Sloman on his skill in integrating ideas from many spiritual sources in his book *Handbook for Humans*. Sloman is known in financial circles for his work on the Delta Phenomenon and Adam Theory..He started a book on markets more than eight years ago but put it aside when he felt directed to prepare the *Handbook*. (He didn't know writing it would take so long), but readers will not be surprised because his book is so thoroughly researched, from Taoism to diets, from evolution to empathy..."

—Vern Barnett, *Kansas City Star*

Nothing
2ND EDITION

James Sloman

NOTHING
Uncovering Our True Nature
2nd edition, 200 pages, $14

"Sitting silently,
Doing nothing,
Spring comes,
And the grass grows by itself."
—Zenrin

What is our true nature? And how do we access it? How do we glimpse it? A facial mirror will do for our face, but what about the mind itself?

Nothing is a mind-mirror which holds up a glass to the mind so that we can begin to observe it. And in that looking, an opening can occur in which life is seen as inherently gracious and rewarding.

"Thank you for *Nothing*...I was overwhelmed."
—*KJ, San Diego*

"*Nothing* came at a time when I was at a peak of dissatisfaction with my life...it worked for me and on me very naturally and easily."
—*AB, South Carolina*

"The single best adjective to describe *Nothing* is 'beautiful'...a superb job."
—*DO, Fort Lauderdale*

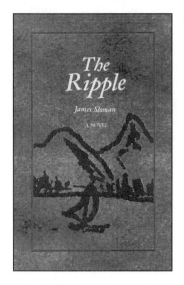

THE RIPPLE
A Mystery Story
Of A Being's Journey
A novel, 400 pages, $15

"*The Ripple,* by James Sloman, shows the broad range of Mr. Sloman's prodigious talent. Set in the overpowering environment of New York City in the 70's (when it was written), *The Ripple* chronicles the breakdown of the human psyche as it strives for autonomy and recognition against the metropolis' spiraling whirlpool of anonymity and powerlessness.

"Sloman creates a darkly tragic yet humorous world where rage and regret dance a tango of bittersweet promise resigned to inevitable defeat. Punkin Miller, a computer programmer who is tormented by fellow workers, shop keepers and women beyond his means, reaches a breaking point...The result is a horrific, heartbreaking and mesmerizing ride as the reader follows Punkin Miller through the maze of mental meltdown, cat and mouse intrigue, and finally, total surrender to the crashing permanence of fate.

"There are valuable lessons to be learned from *The Ripple* about the human condition. But make no mistake. *The Ripple* is a dark journey through the underside of the beast, and though redemption is found at last, the price is the loss of a soul."

—Michael Gottlieb, author of *Squeeze Play*

AFFECTING
OUR REALITY
Chicago Talk Series
Set of 4 cassettes, $22

Topics of Discussion:

- Finding your calling in life
- The role of play in vision
- Looking at what's real
- Loving, accepting ourselves
- Surrender and freedom
- The paradox of feelings
- Everything as a gift
- Life as mystery and magic

"A kind and soothing voice...I felt a sense of self-awareness, a warmth, a glow, a knowledge I've known before only I don't know where...a real insight to life and living."

—*S.K., Miami, FL*

"Thank you...wonderful!"

—*J.M., St. Louis, MO*

"So good...excellent!"

—*C.C., Monterey, CA*

SONGS FROM THE BOTTOM OF THE SEA

18 songs, voice & guitar

Set of 2 CDs, $22

"Jackpot!"

"Now, perhaps more than ever, it seems that you can't swing a Martin steel-string without hitting a folk singer. But one of the great things about the persistence and popularity of singer-songwriter types is that every so often a new voice comes along that reminds us that folk singers can still be legit and likeable even in the '90s.

"In the vast sea of singer/songwriters, Sloman's rich, clear, well-recorded voice stands out...

"There's plenty here for folkies and non-folk fans alike to grab. In addition to his use of abundantly vivid personal details and storytelling and songwriting tactics ("Charlie"), Sloman's most surprising trick could be his rewrites of cover songs like "The Night They Drove Old Dixie Down" or "Summertime," where he gets the words down right but embellishes and distends the music, adding his own melody underneath to create a completely new song that's respectful and appreciative of the original, but fresh and vital nonetheless."

—*CMJ New Music Report*

TO PLACE AN ORDER:

Call: 800-838-7360

Abroad: 707-838-6200

Or mail the order form with your
check to OceanBlue Publishing

*SHIPPING & HANDLING

In the US, add $4 shipping for
first item, $1 for each additional
item. Express and international,
please call for shipping.

www.ocean-blue.com

OceanBlue Publishing
98 Main Street
Tiburon, CA 94920

ITEM	QTY	PRICE	AMOUNT
May You Be Happy		$12	
Handbook for Humans		$24	
Nothing		$14	
The Ripple		$15	
Affecting Our Reality set		$22	
Songs From....Sea set		$22	

Subtotal _____

CA residents add 7.5% tax _____

Shipping* _____

Total Enclosed _____

Name _____

Address _____

CityStateZip _____

DayPhone/e-mail _____